English Jurisprudence:

On Complicity (Volum-01)

...Jurist AKG

Contents

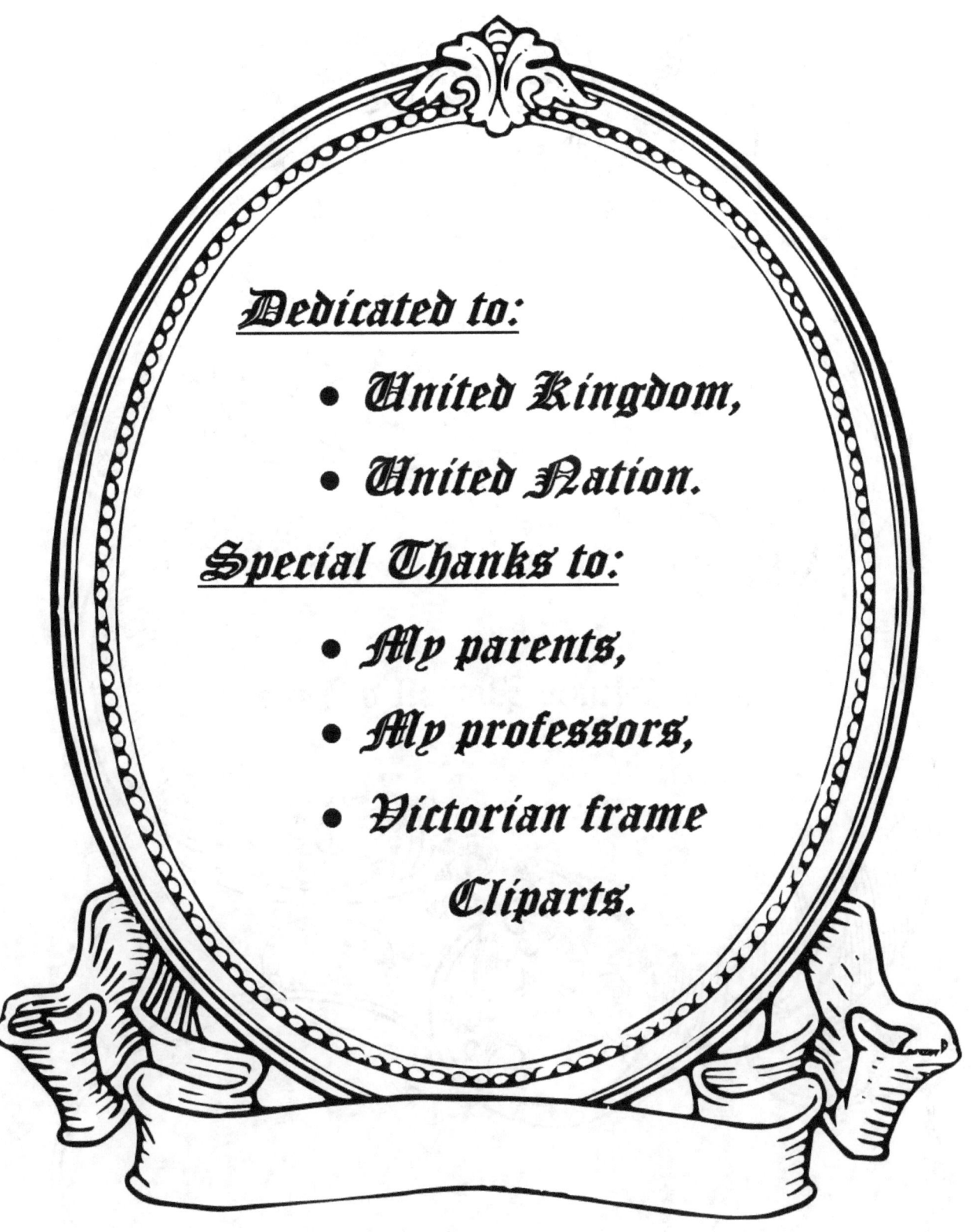

Dedicated to:

- *United Kingdom,*
- *United Nation.*

Special Thanks to:

- *My parents,*
- *My professors,*
- *Victorian frame Cliparts.*

Case Study: Powell v Jogee

Issue:-

Deciding guilty mind of secondary liability is not left as easy as deciding guilty mind of any other crime, after the Supreme Court of United Kingdom (UKSC) pronounce its judgment on R v Jogee & R v Ruddock. Assistance or encouragement is the crucial thing to be decided to identify the intention of secondary party. The question remains about the meaning of encouragement because in R v Jogee, UKSC said that the secondary party (Jogee) is not liable because there was no knowledge or intention that the Principal (Hirsi) is going to stab the victim (Fyfe), but Jogee & Hirsi took dutch courage before doing the murder & was highly intoxicated and aggressive at the time of murder along with Jogee encouraged to Hirshi smash the drink bottle at the head of Fyfe which can also be considered as encouragement.

Case Study: R v Jogee & R v Ruddock:-

ISSUE:- The question of law was whether the common law took a wrong turning in two cases, Chan Wing-Siu v The Queen and Regina v Powell and English.

FACTS:- The appellant Jogee was convicted at Nottingham Crown Court of the murder of Paul Fyfe. Mr Fyfe was the boyfriend of Naomi Reid and he was stabbed to death in the hallway of her home in the early hours of 10 June 2011 by the appellant's co-defendant, Mohammed Hirsi. Hirsi was convicted of murder. The appellant and Hirsi spent the previous evening at various places, taking drink and drugs. They became increasingly intoxicated and increasingly aggressive. Shortly before midnight they arrived at Ms Reid's house. She told them to leave and They left but Hirsi returned and was there when Mr Fyfe arrived. Hirsi entered the house and there was an angry confrontation between him and Mr Fyfe. The appellant was outside with a bottle and shouting to Hirsi to do something to Mr Fyfe and at one stage the appellant came to the door and threatened to smash the bottle over Mr Fyfe's head. The fatal stabbing was done by Hirsi with a knife which he took from the kitchen. The judge directed the jury that the appellant was guilty of murder if he took part in the attack on Mr Fyfe and realised that it was possible that Hirsi might use the knife with intent to cause serious harm. The appellant Ruddock was convicted in the Circuit Court at Montego Bay, Jamaica, of the murder of Peter Robinson. The appellant's co-defendant, Hudson, pleaded guilty to the murder. Mr Robinson was a taxi driver and the prosecution's case was that the murder was committed in the course of robbing him of his station wagon. The police evidence was that the appellant made a statement under caution which amounted to an admission that he was involved in committing the robbery and that he was present when Hudson killed the victim by cutting his throat but a denial that the appellant was responsible for the killing. The judge directed the jury that Ruddock was guilty of murder if he took part in the robbery and knew that there was a possibility that Hudson might intend to kill the victim.

JUDGMENT:- The unanimous conclusion of the court is that Chan Wing-Siu and Powell and English did take a wrong turning and these appeals should therefore be allowed. The correct rule is that foresight is simply evidence, albeit sometimes strong evidence, of intent to assist or encourage, which is the proper mental element for establishing secondary liability.

Joint Enterprise Doctrine:-

This has developed to address these kind of eventualities and the basic principle governing joint enterprise liability which is now understood as same as accessoryship. It deals with three situations:

- **_Firstly,_** liability for unforeseen consequences of executing the joint enterprise where an unexpected consequence arises from the execution of the joint enterprise. In this case, the unforeseen consequence was murder of Fyfe by Hisrhi.

- *Secondly,* Liability for accidental deviations in the execution of the joint enterprise where P accidentally deviates in the execution of the joint enterprise. In this case, P stabbed Fyfe which is considered as accidental deviation because Jogee was saying to smash the bottle over Fyfe's head. It is evident that murder was not planned.
- *Thirdly,* Liability for deliberate deviations in the execution of the joint enterprise. In this case, what P did was a deliberate deviation. Jogee was encouraging to smash the bottle over Fyfe's head, but P deliberately stabbed him.

Accessories and Abettors Act 1861:-

Section 8 states that whosoever shall aid, abet, counsel or procure the commission of any indictable offence shall be liable to be tried, indicted, and punished as a principal offender. Accessory to an offence is guilty of the substantive offence, rather than – in the case of conspiracy, an accessory to an offence is guilty of the substantive offence, rather than – in the case of conspiracy. Here, in this case Jogee is accessory & Hirshi is the principal. Jogee & Hirshi jointly arrived at the house of Fyfe where Jogee encouraged P to smash the bottle over Fyfe's head which is a wrongful act, but Hirshi did something different. He stabbed Fyfe about which Jogee did not have any prior knowledge or he did not encouraged for stabbing. This issue has been considered by UKSC very firmly because Jogee did encouraged, but his word or intention to hurt Fyfe was different which than the act of Hirshi.

Elements of accessoryship:-

Aiding, abetting, counselling or procuring is the most important concepts which can be reproduced into to two: encouraging or assisting. Aid means to help or assist. Abet involves instigation or encouragement. Counsel implies advising or urging. Procure means to persuade or cause. Actus reus or P must have committed an offence. A's liability does not derive from what A has done but what P has done. Here, in this case, Jogee encouraged Hirshi and advised to smash the bottle over Fyfe's head, but Hirshi stabbed him to death. Definitely, Jogee abet & counsel Hirshi. The question remains here that if A's liability has to be decided by the act of P and not from A's activity, then Jogee is liable for murder because Hirshi as P murdered Fyfe, even though Jogee had no knowledge that Hirshi could stab Fyfe which is contrary to the principle of communication of causation.

Communication & causation:-

The principle of communication & causation says that if the basis upon which A is charged is an act of encouragement, this has to be communicated to the principal. If, therefore, P does not hear or read the words of encouragement, A cannot be charged as an accessory on the basis of that act alone. Direct causal connection between the words of encouragement and the commission of the offence requires. Here, in this case, Jogee threatened to smash the bottle over Fyfe's head, but Hirshi stabbed him. So, P did something different than A's words of encouragement. Considering which it can be said that Jogee cannot be liable as an accessory for murder of Fyfe.

Intention to assist or encourage:-

To remove the confusion of communication &causation principle mens rea must be decided. The mens rea requirement in complicity is twofold:

- *Firstly,* it indicates the importance that A knows, rather than simply suspects that their conduct will assist or encourage the commission of an offence. Here, in this case, A had neither any knowledge that P could pick up a knife & stab Fyfe nor could ever imagine about that. So, the first criteria of mens rea of complicity are not fulfilled here for Jogee.
- *Secondly,* Liability of accessories for unforeseen consequences arises when A, who supplies P with an article useful in the commission of an offence but

P deliberately, commits another offence. Here, in this case, Jogee did not supply any article to commit the crime. If we consider that jogee threatened to smash the bottle over Fyfe's head, even then also he did not supplied any article. Whatever, P did, that was deliberate. So, we can easily separate Jogee form the liability of complicity.

Withdrawal:-

Another difficult area is withdrawal. It was considered that once having signed up to assisting or encouraging the commission of a criminal offence, it is nevertheless possible for A to withdraw their assistance and/or encouragement and thus escape liability as an accessory to that offence and A may remain liable for any inchoate offence, such as conspiracy, which they may have committed. In this case, there is no question of withdrawal communicated between the P & the A. so, this is not relevant here.

R v Powell; English:-

Lord Steyn in R v Powell; English said that in order to deal with this important social problem, the accessory principle is needed and cannot be abolished or relaxed. Powell and Daniels, went to purchase drugs from a drug dealer, but having gone to his house for that purpose, the drug dealer was shot dead when he came to the door. The Crown was unable to prove which of the three men fired the gun that killed the drug dealer. The defence argued that this meant that all three must be acquitted since two of them did not pull the trigger. This is highly contradictory to the adversarial litigation system because the standard of proof is proof beyond doubt. If prosecution fails to prove who shot the drug dealer, then everyone related to the crime must be acquitted.

Woolmington v DPP:-

The House of Lords had to consider whether the fact that the actus reus was satisfied meant that the burden was placed on A to prove that the killing was an accident. The famous conclusion it reached was that the burden of proof did not pass to A, and never would. People are assumed innocent until proven guilty. This means that in respect of all the elements of all offences the burden of proof is on the prosecution. So with respect to the actus reus the prosecution must do the proving, and it must prove every bit of the actus reus. Again, with respect to the mens rea, the prosecution must do all the proving. Finally, with respect to defences, again the prosecution must do the disproving. The prosecution must prove each and every element of the offence 'beyond reasonable doubt'.

R v Jogee; Ruddock:-

The Supreme Court agreed that in cases of joint enterprise in murder the contemplation basis for liability established in Chan Wing Siu and approved in Powell was a wrong turning. It was insufficient that the secondary party contemplated that the principal might commit murder. Jogee was retried at Leicester Crown Court. His conviction was quashed and replaced by a conviction for manslaughter. The jury found that there was insufficient evidence that the defendant intended to encourage the principal to kill or cause serious injury. There was sufficient evidence that he intended to encourage a lesser harm for which a conviction for manslaughter is proper. Chan Wing-Siu; Rv Powell; & R v English held that in the kind of situation described, the mental element required of the secondary party of D2 is simply that he foresaw the possibility that D1 might commit crime B. The conclusion of this court is that they did take a wrong turning in their reasoning, even if the outcome might well have been the same if the error had not been made. Sometimes the encouragement or assistance is given to a specific crime, and sometimes to a range of crimes, one of which is committed which either will suffice. Sometimes the encouragement or assistance involves an agreement between the parties, but in other cases it takes the form of more or less spontaneous joining in a criminal enterprise which either will suffice. Intention to assist is not the same as desiring the crime to be committed. In many cases, the intention to assist will be co-terminous with the intention which sometimes are conditional that crime committed by B. The error was to treat foresight of crime B as automatic authorisation of intent to assist or encourage on the part of A as decided in Chan Wing-Siu and Reg; R v Powell; R v English.

The Present Cases Do Not Decide:-

There are some rules which must not be altered, are as follows:

- *First,* a person who joins in a crime which any reasonable person would realise involves a risk of harm, and death results, is guilty at least of manslaughter. Here, Jogee is a reasonable man with no mental disability. He involved with Hirshi to injure or bring harm to Fyfe. So, Jogee must be liable for at-least manslaughter in his intention differs with the intention of Hirshi.
- *Secondly,* a person who intentionally encourages or assists the commission of a crime is as guilty as the person who physically commits it. Here, in this case the only exception was that that Jogee drank a lot, but giving Dutch courage to do a crime cannot be treated as any defence. So, he must be guilty for manslaughter.
- *Thirdly,* it is open to a jury to infer intentional encouragement or assistance. It is a commonplace for juries to have to decide what inferences they can properly draw about intention from an accused person's behaviour and what he knew. Jury was very certain that Jogee must be convicted for manslaughter.

Did Previous Cases Really Turned Wrong:-

The main ratio was laid down in Powell's case following the ratio of Chan Wing Siu. Powell's ratio did take a wrong turn in two ways:

- *Firstly,* according to Woolmington v DPP the prosecution has to prove & do disprove all the charges in favor or against of his/her client. In this case it was not proved that who committed the crime. So, punishment for murder would be inappropriate here.
- *Secondly,* if the prosecution fails to prove the main principal, then there is a difficulty to decide the liability of accessories. What knowledge accessory had or whether they supported that or there was any accidental deviation or any withdrawal present or not.

Conclusion:-

We can conclude certainly that previous cases did take wrong turning which has firmly been overruled in R v jogee; Ruddock.

References:-

- *https://www.bailii.org/*
- *https://www.supremecourt.uk/decided-cases/*
- *https://www.jcpc.uk/decided-cases/index.html*

<u>Anything to note?</u>

Order Backed by Threats
(OBT) & Morality in law

Issue:-

Austin said that Order Backed by Threats (OBT) has no objective morality and people obey because of habitual obedience. Where there is no morality, there cannot be any habitual obedience. In the following case study, it is evident that sometimes OBT requires removing crime to have a peaceful society, but court plays always a great role to bring morality in law.

R v Jogee & R v Ruddock:-

ISSUE:- The question of law was whether the common law took a wrong turning in two cases, Chan Wing-Siu v The Queen [1985 1 AC 168 and Regina v Powell and English [1999] 1 AC 1.

FACTS:- The appellant Jogee was convicted at Nottingham Crown Court of the murder of Paul Fyfe. Mr Fyfe was the boyfriend of Naomi Reid and he was stabbed to death in the hallway of her home in the early hours of 10 June 2011 by the appellant's co-defendant, Mohammed Hirsi. Hirsi was convicted of murder. The appellant and Hirsi spent the previous evening at various places, taking drink and drugs. They became increasingly intoxicated and increasingly aggressive. Shortly before midnight they arrived at Ms Reid's house. She told them to leave and They left but Hirsi returned and was there when Mr Fyfe arrived. Hirsi entered the house and there was an angry confrontation between him and Mr Fyfe. The appellant was outside with a bottle and shouting to Hirsi to do something to Mr Fyfe and at one stage the appellant came to the door and threatened to smash the bottle over Mr Fyfe's head. The fatal stabbing was done by Hirsi with a knife which he took from the kitchen. The judge directed the jury that the appellant was guilty of murder if he took part in the attack on Mr Fyfe and realised that it was possible that Hirsi might use the knife with intent to cause serious harm. The appellant Ruddock was convicted in the Circuit Court at Montego Bay, Jamaica, of the murder of Peter Robinson. The appellant's co-defendant, Hudson, pleaded guilty to the murder. Mr Robinson was a taxi driver and the prosecution's case was that the murder was committed in the course of robbing him of his station wagon. The police evidence was that the appellant made a statement under caution which amounted to an admission that he was involved in committing the robbery and that he was present when Hudson killed the victim by cutting his throat but a denial that the appellant was responsible for the killing. The judge directed the jury that Ruddock was guilty of murder if he took part in the robbery and knew that there was a possibility that Hudson might intend to kill the victim.

JUDGMENT:- The unanimous conclusion of the court is that Chan Wing-Siu and Powell and English did take a wrong turning and these appeals should therefore be allowed. The correct rule is that foresight is simply evidence, albeit sometimes strong evidence, of intent to assist or encourage, which is the proper mental element for establishing secondary liability.

T. Hobbes:-

Thomas Hobbes believed in Liberalism. He was the invader of Leviathan. Theory of legitimacy means why subject should show obedience to Sovereign authority. He described Sovereign authority as nature of state. Sometime this nature of state is egoistic which causes war of all on all. The Theory of Materialist on foundation emphasized on scientific view of humans and their place in the world. To control this egoistic nature and to ensure the scientific view of human being and their place in world, the Treaty of Westphalia sovereignty with particular territory by which every sovereign become nation state with a particular territory.

It cannot be denied that state sometimes became egoistic which causes many wars at past decades. This case is the best answer of the statement made by Hobbes that subject should show obedience to Sovereign authority. Unless secondary liability are not punished by sovereign power which is exercised through courts & legislated through Parliament, then it would became a profession for some people whom we call the accessories (A). They became part of joint enterprise liability with intention to bring harm or injury through others named principal (P), but escape from punishment. Chag Wing Siu, English, Powell's case denotes that it took a wrong turn because sovereign authority was there, but it did not consider that whether the secondary part has any knowledge about the crime or not. This situation can raise frustration & increase crime rate because innocent people can go punished. This gray area has been removed in the case of Jogee & Ruddock that it was unknown to the secondary party that the P is going take a knife from the kitchen & going to stab Fyfe. He encouraged in different ways, for example, to smash the bottle over Fyfe's head, but he never spoke anything about stabbing the victim. If this person goes punished for murder, then he will lose faith from justice system which will frustrate him & increase criminality in him. The UKSC played a great role here to bring morality in law by deciding that A must be punished for that particular crime which he did, i e, manslaughter. When law regulates through morality, then habitual obedience bring justice & pleasure to the society.

Austin:-

According to Austin the habit of obedience are rules of terror which treats law as obligation and its Subjects are being obliged to obey the law made by the ruler. Austin mainly worked on general jurisprudence and analytical jurisprudence. He speaks about prevading Notions which includes Law, legal right, legal duty, and legal validity. He treated this doctrine of OBT as Legal formalism which means narrow approach of role of law. Command which is expressed with sanctions, but this has some exceptions including repealing any law, declarative law, imperfect law.

Professor Cotterrell: Sovereignty exists when two conditions are satisfied:

- Firstly, bulk of the society is in a habit of obedience to a common superior and,
- Secondly, that individual or body is not, itself, in a habit of obedience to a determinate human superior.

According to him Bentham and Austin's legal theory recognised the reality of the modern state as a massive organisation of power. It tried to show the relationship of law with this centralised and extensive power structure. Austin's theory was devoted to science of law, and not the theory of law as means the science of legislation. The coercive structure of a law shows that there are several things to follow from governmental view of law like duties are more fundamental than rights. Professor Cotterrell says that the individual's ability to make specific claims on others through the legal system is derivative from the law's commands with which we cannot agree because it is not always true because when there is no law, people are to do anything or to claim anything as their right. He described Austin's command theory produces its result analytically that sanctions are analytically essential to laws, whether or not they are sociologically necessary. Again, this statement is non-agreeable because if any law is not necessary for the society, then that law will as unused. Austin's theory of smallest chance of the smallest evil encompasses a wide range of possible sanctions from monetary sanction to fine or imprisonment and so on.

Contradicting with Austin:- It is true that sometimes laws are rules of terror which is necessary to have a peaceful society. This case found that previous cases means Chag Wing Siu, English, Powell's took a wrong turn. The gray area has been removed in the case of Jogee & Ruddock that it was unknown to the secondary party that the P is going take a knife from the kitchen & going to stab Fyfe. He encouraged in different ways, for example, to smash the bottle over Fyfe's head, but he never spoke anything about stabbing the victim. If there were no rules of terror, then anyone will bring harm to others & will go unpunished. Human brain is made out of three parts. Two of which developed from animal brain & one part called cognition develop is their unique development which developed them as rational or reasonable being. Reasonability says that bringing harm or injury to others are wrongful acts because no-one can live alone in one planet. To become rational being, everyone needs to develop cognition which can easy be developing through education by developing critical thinking & by hard way of gaining experience. Gaining experience or education which develop critical thinking is not easy accessible for everyone. There we need some rules of terror which include morality.

Contradicting Professor Cotterrell:- Professor said that it is true that sovereign exists where bulk of the society is in a habit of obedience to a common superior, but it is not at all true that that individual or body is not, itself, in a habit of obedience to a determinate human superior. It has two reasons, are as follows:

- King cannot do any wrong because he does his works always through someone. The primary source of work has always been supplied to him. He never goes to collect information directly. He decides what to do on the basis of that information. So, he cannot liable for the wrong decision taken by him, depending upon the wrong information provided to him.

- If the king take bad decision then he is can be held also liable from 17th century. Historically, at Stuart England the two tier legal systems were in force mean the English Common law & the royal prerogative by which king tortured at the Star Chamber. At His Majesty King Charles-I's tyranny regime, jailor refused to release prisoners arrested arbitrarily because they were there with King's authority & the Charles forced to sign a royal restraining order containing rights for all English man, but the Star Chamber judges found alternative ways about taxes with Brutus physical punishment for treason. At that period, no Cab Rank Rule was there when John cook took the case against Charles to prosecute tyranny. The only question of law related to this case was that in England the source of the law is the king & how could the source of law be prosecuted by the law. He interpreted that King is not an individual, but an office & the hold of that office he had to govern by & according to the laws of the land and not otherwise. On January 20, 1649 Charles brought to Westminster hall court room from the backdoor where Oliver Cromwell prosecuted the case and from then the source of the English law became subject to the law. Finally, Charles Stuart was condemned to death by the death warrant of a king issued by court that signed by 59 Soldiers, Alderman, Judges at Whitehall for the execution.

This case of King Charles Stuart changed the entire view of English Legal System, but these concepts are not relevant nowadays, because King or Queen is ceremonial now. We have Parliament to check the activities of executive by ministerial accountability & legislate laws. We have judicial review to check executive actions & Parliament to some extent because where legislation conflicts with constitutional principle that are generally be set aside by the court according to the principle of *ultra vires* which can also be used to check actions of executives.

Bentham:-

Bentham was mainly focused on what law ought to be according to the responsibility & duty of government. His work on Utilitarianism speaks that sacred truth or maximum satisfaction in long run. The government must make such laws thorough which the state and its citizens and other members can achieve highest happiness at their life. Professor Cotterrell says that limitations on sovereign power are legal which Bentham suggests that some of these limitations leges in principem. He recognises that leges in principem, like all other laws, must derive from the sovereign but his explanations of how the sovereign can bind itself are far from satisfactory, relying on suggestions about the invocation of external pressures of popular opinion, religious or moral sanctions, or international relations.

Professor, Bentham & Cotterrell are both correctly identified that if law is esstial to maintain our human rights, then to maximise that happiness we need to have positive & negative form of rights. Comparing with this case, intention to harm or injure others must be prohibited as negative rights, but when there was no intention expressed by Jogee to bring harm or injure Fyfe with knife, then punishing him for that would be unlawful, but may be not with knife, Jogee wanted to bring harm to Fyfe. So, manslaughter is the best charge to be brought against him which is also a negative right requires for the maximization of happiness, as professor Bentham & Cotterrell said. OBT requires protecting the society & upholding the liberty, but with morality as Bentham argued for maximisation of happiness.

H.L.A. Hart:-

The Conception of Law introduced the Rule of recognition which says that the internal points of view of law are the acceptance of social practice which is not unproblematic. Austin is raising his point here that the societal acceptance is habitual obedience backed by threats. Indeed, we cannot disagree with Austin here because crime happens for two reasons mainly:

- Violation of freedom, Equality, Liberty for which people ultimately inclined to civil wars; &
- Emotion when causes mental disorder, then people became tyrannical and/or corrupted.

The External point of view of the Rule of recognition deals with why anyone would accept the rule of recognition and no acceptance of social practice without justifying causes. Professor Hart provide chess example which he termed as "The theory of Paradox of Rule-Following". This says that the rules of Chess are not restricted every time. Like one can find & use new moves, new interpretation of rule can be imported at law. He discussed that the doctrine of Linguistic Method or Linguistic Philosophy are two kinds,

- Firstly, Primary means subjects are being obliged, forced and duty Imposing; &
- Secondly, being under an obligation what is ought. How Idea of Obligation can cure the Pre-Legal or social defects which are static, inefficient, uncertain and this was missed by Austin.

Furthermore, the Rule of recognition of Hart speaks about the Semantic Sting means no adequate account of law can be based on a description solely of how people speak. If we take that into account, then every law must be just, fair and reasonable which include morality, even if it is backed by sovereign threats. The Rule of Recognition or The Ultimate Rule says that Austin said about tacit consent of OBT theory. Penumbra cases or where there is an uncertainty in case or in an issue in question about what the law requires, that must be decided by morality to give specific interpretation about the just, fair and reasonableness of the law which Austin's OBT theory missed.

In the case Powell or English, there was a chance to raise of frustration throughout the country along with a chance to raise criminality because when law starts to injustice, then people got frustrated with the law & take the law in their hand which raises crime, but here no such situation is going to arise because English laws are strong enough to acknowledge & deal with its mistakes and the R v Jogee and/or R v Ruddock are the best example of that.

Dworkin:-

Dworkin was the founder of doctrine of Interpretation. This theory has three stages of interpretation, are as follows: Pre-Interpretative means where no attitude is stuck towards the value of the rule. Austin's theory of OBT is stuck here. According to Austin, the rule uses its final wordings on its subjects, but according to Dworkin's second stage of interpretation theory we can find that the Interpretative stage is for Questioning, differing, doing argument for the problem in question which most of its time Fold back into itself & effect of changing the original rule through judicial legislation which we call Post-Interpretative stage. The ground of Law must be social practice with moral force of law. Without morality, there cannot be any law.

If we consider this case in light of the interpretation theory of Dworkin, we can find that pre-interpretation theory deals with punishment of secondary liability is the same as principal which was decided in R v Powell or English or other cases, although the prosecution fails to prove beyond all reasonable doubt that what was the intention of the secondary party. The Interpretative stage states that this point of law had been challenged at court through the case of R v Jogee & Ruddock. Finally, the post-interpretative stage changed the original rule by deciding that Jogee had no same intention as the Principal, so he must not be punished for murder.

Finnis:-

The Natural Law Theory of Finnis says that realists deal with skepticism which means moral values & principles do exists. As cognitivists he thinks that the human must know moral values & principles to judge what just expressions of our emotional attitudes are. His Natural Fallacy says that natural rights are that what is ought to be. Here, he is differing with Austin's theory of OBT because if principles are to be judged in the light of what is ought to be, then order backed by threats of sovereignty cannot fail to recognize morality in law.

As decided in this case that Jogee cannot be punished for murder because he had no knowledge or intention to bring harm or injury to Fyfe through knife, but he must be punished for manslaughter because he wanted bring harm or injury by smashing the bottle at Fyfe's head. This is a fit case to describe the thinking of both Finnis & Austin that natural law or OBT contain morality in itself.

Fuller:-

Fuller mainly focused on morality or the Rule of law. His theory of rule of law or morality gives birth to a new theory, the Procedural Natural Law theory. This theory says about the morally sound aspects of governing by rules. The Procedural Natural Law theory or Substantive law requires assessing them with requirement of law-making and administration purposes. Professor Cotterrell says that Austin's theory is not a theory of the Rule of Law or of government subject to law. It is a theory of the 'rule of men' or of government using law as an instrument of power and such a view may be considered realistic or merely cynical. But it is, in its broad outlines, essentially coherent. Here I am highly disagreeing with professor Cotterrell because rule of law means widely accepted & tested community values. The nature provided us a user model of norms or laws which we call cognition. So, men has to find out what is ought & what is ought not right by using their cognitive thinking which if a gift of nature to human being only. Natural law deals with oughtness, then rule of law cannot be identified as rule of men only because it contains morality in itself.

Here, in this case, an injustice was done in the case of Powell & English which was identified by the UKSC in R v Jogee & Ruddock. So, UKSC corrected the wrong turn took at Powell & English by using the user model of norms & laws gifted by nature to us means the cognitive thinking. So, we cannot say that rule of law means rule of men government using law as an instrument of power.

Conclusion:-

Where there is no morality, there cannot be any habitual obedience. Historically, when there is excess of immorality done by any ruler, but English Common Law is the greatest gift of this nation to the world to protect society & defend liberty along with civil war because common people went on to civil war which ended by bringing revolutionary changes at the society.

References:-

- https://treasuryofenglishlaws.wordpress.com/2019/04/10/obt-morality-in-law/

<u>Anything to note?</u>

Liberalism & The Law

Issue:-

Liberalism speaks about freedom and equality. According to the principles of utilitarianism, law must ensure maximum happiness to its people by treating everyone equally. This can only be achieved when law strictly consider morality into it. This case defines & upheld the morality in law properly by deciding that it is immoral to hold someone guilty for murder when there was no knowledge & intention is present.

R v Jogee & R v Ruddock:-

ISSUE:- The question of law was whether the common law took a wrong turning in two cases, Chan Wing Siu v The Queen and Regina v Powell and English.

FACTS:- The appellant Jogee was convicted at Nottingham Crown Court of the murder of Paul Fyfe. Mr Fyfe was the boyfriend of Naomi Reid and he was stabbed to death in the hallway of her home in the early hours of 10 June 2011 by the appellant's co-defendant, Mohammed Hirsi. Hirsi was convicted of murder. The appellant and Hirsi spent the previous evening at various places, taking drink and drugs. They became increasingly intoxicated and increasingly aggressive. Shortly before midnight they arrived at Ms Reid's house. She told them to leave and they left but Hirsi returned and was there when Mr Fyfe arrived. Hirsi entered the house and there was an angry confrontation between him and Mr Fyfe. The appellant was outside with a bottle and shouting to Hirsi to do something to Mr Fyfe and at one stage the appellant came to the door and threatened to smash the bottle over Mr Fyfe's head. The fatal stabbing was done by Hirsi with a knife which he took from the kitchen. The judge directed the jury that the appellant was guilty of murder if he took part in the attack on Mr Fyfe and realised that it was possible that Hirsi might use the knife with intent to cause serious harm. The appellant Ruddock was convicted in the Circuit Court at Montego Bay, Jamaica, of the murder of Peter Robinson. The appellant's co-defendant, Hudson, pleaded guilty to the murder. Mr Robinson was a taxi driver and the prosecution's case was that the murder was committed in the course of robbing him of his station wagon. The police evidence was that the appellant made a statement under caution which amounted to an admission that he was involved in committing the robbery and that he was present when Hudson killed the victim by cutting his throat but a denial that the appellant was responsible for the killing. The judge directed the jury that Ruddock was guilty of murder if he took part in the robbery and knew that there was a possibility that Hudson might intend to kill the victim.

JUDGMENT:- The unanimous conclusion of the court is that Chan Wing-Siu and Powell and English did take a wrong turning and these appeals should therefore be allowed. The correct rule is that foresight is simply evidence, albeit sometimes strong evidence, of intent to assist or encourage, which is the proper mental element for establishing secondary liability.

Liberalism:-

Bentham was the author of utilitarianism which is a moral theory. This theory was developed by Bentham, depending on what law ought to be. According to utilitarianism everyone must be free to bargain without any constrains created by inequalities of bargain power. Bentham, said where there are inequalities, states must think to remove that inequality of bargaining power and must bring happiness back to everyone by ensuring their rights. This brings the growth of liberalism says that each man to count as one and no-one to count for more than one and economy. If the state starts to count every person as one, then that is the best path to bring equality in that society.

Here, in this case, an inequality of bargain power was present that even though the prosecution fails to prove who killed the drug dealer, but the House of Lords held Powell & English guilty for the offence. In this way, happiness cannot be achieved. This is what Austin and Thomas Hobbes said that law means command backed by sovereign which does not contain any morality in it. Everyone obeys law because of habitual obedience which they termed as inequalities in bargaining power, but our English laws are well-equipped to correct its mistakes. In the case of R v Jogee, Jogee was counted as one person & not more than one, maybe he was part of a joint enterprise. In Powell & English, Principal and Accessory were treated as one which was a violation to the principles of liberty found by Bentham. UKSC count Jogee means the Accessory separate from the Principle which brings the most happiness in our English society by bringing equality to our justice system and this removed the inequality of bargaining power from the laws of secondary liability.

Rule-Utilitarianism:-

This speaks that every people have their rights which must be guaranteed & must have capacity to exercise them, when needed. As lawyers explain that these rights are legal rights because unless right is guaranteed by law, no-one cares for it. Moreover, when the right is guaranteed by law, then also people not step aside from encroaching upon another's right. This is because human two parts of human brain are evolved from animal brain and the rational or cognitive development part has been evolved separately. Still, we cannot 100% with lawyer's statement of rule-utilitarianism are only legal rights because some people are also there who uphold other rights first than theirs, but we cannot disagree with Bentham that yes, every people have their rights for their survival.

Here, in this case, we can find that Jogee has a right that he had no knowledge or intention to hurt or injure Fyfe by knife. So, he must not be tried or held guilty for murder. His right to be tried for the relevant crime must be protected & guarded legally and fir this reason lawyers argue this right of rule-utilitarianism as legal right, even though Parliament is also protecting rights of people by enacting statutes. Powell & English's case failed to recognise the right of rule-utilitarianism properly, but UKSC in Jogee decided it correctly that both Jogee & Fyfe's rights must be protected. Maybe Jogee did wanted to murder Fyfe with knife, but he encouraged to smash the bottle over Fyfe's head. Fyfe's rights are also needs to be protected. So, this case is fit case to bring charges of manslaughter against Jogee.

Equality:-

Bernard Williams argues that equality has a special meaning in morality to strike at unjustified statuses and hierarchies. One of the reasons we approve of 'equality of opportunity' is that we think that everyone, because of their common humanity, should have the same sorts of chances in life, even though some cannot, take them up. There are two kind of criticism of this thinking of equality:

- Firstly, more freedom and less equality. They say they oppose equality because it is 'uneconomic' and stifles human endeavour, enterprise and creativity.
- Secondly, there are more equality and less freedom, and these people are usually for more state support and intervention, particularly in the real marketplace.

This criticism of equality is not exhaustive to deal with every situation. For example, here, in this case, we cannot find any situation relating to more freedom & less quality relating to uneconomic or stifles human endeavour, enterprise and creativity. Freedom concerns in this case are that that an accessory must be tried for the committed offence & not more than that which Bentham indicates to reach maximum happiness in the society. Secondly, no question of marketplace lies in this case. So, these two criticisms that provided by Bernard Williams are very narrow in nature, comparing the principle of utilitarianism provided by Bentham.

Criticism:-

There are many criticisms available against utilitarianism, are as follows:

Dontology:- Dontology which says that the morality of an action should be based on whether that action itself is right or wrong under a series of rules, rather than based on the consequences of the action. This is a question of moral disagreement. One thing must be noticed that if we don't measure the consequences of actions, we can never define the _mens rea_. Series of rules developed depeding upon circumstances. Nature did not provide us any user manual of laws or norms, but it gave us cognition to tackle this kind of situation. When crime will happen, guilty mind which developed through cognitive development must decide through the series of circumstances which start to form rules. For example, considering this case, we can say that secondary liability was a very difficult area to find out the exact _mens rea_ until the decision of R V Jogee & Ruddock. There was a series of rules including both statues & precedents, but they failed to count one man as one because the sole rule for secondary liability was that that the accessory must be charged & held guilty for the same amount of offence of the principle of the joint enterprise. Then these rules are treating two or more accessories are one like its principle. Here, donology fails because if these rules were not corrected by UKSC, then that would increase crime & could never be able to achieve maximum happiness for the society as whole.

Separateness:- As John Rawl's criticizes that this theory is failing to take separateness of persons seriously. The central weaknesses of Utilitarianism or It cannot take the individual perspective into account with which I cannot agree totally. For example, in the case of Powell & English, UKHL considered the liability of accessory same as principal, but it does not mean that it is the failure of the theory because in the later case R v Jogee, UKSC decided that the knowledge & intention of crime made jointly must be identified correctly. Here, the principle murdered through a knife, but the accessory never expressed a single word about the knife, rather he was encouraging to smash the head of Fyfe by bottle. So, it is presumed that UKSC interpreted the theory correctly and treated the principle & accessory as one person and not more than one while deciding the case.

Kentian notion:- Some jurists says that the essential Liberal Notion is based on Kentian notion of person, free will, ability to make choice, plan for one's life. This cannot treated as criticism because indeed, to ensure maximum happiness the notion of person, free will, ability to make choice, plan for one's life must be taken into account. For example, in this case, to maximise the happiness of the society two things must be done:

- Wrongful act must be prohibited means bringing harm or injury to others with conscious mind is prohibited under English law; &
- Right punishment for right crime means as decided in Jogee that principal & accessory's intention & knowledge must be same for the crime which they are going to do.

The Hart-Devlin debate:- This debate says that liberty is immoral in lack of self-discipline, disrespectful to people or life, indulge, tasteless. I am strongly disagreeing with this statement that liberty is immoral. Liberty means freedom and equality which is not different than morality. Liberty ensures equality which brings respect towards the feelings of others. Liberty definitely indulge people, but if that indulgence encroach upon other's rights, then the cases turns and liberty starts prevent that person who being indulge by it encroached on another's right, also it start to protect the right of the victim. Indulgence is not always bad. Finally, freedom and equality can make everything alive by removing the curtain under which it was put which some jurists criticized as tasteless. This tastelessness can be used to protect human rights. When people will know everything behind the curtain, then they will refrain from the bad which will provide a healthy society. Except the Kentian Liberal notion, any other criticism cannot stand again utilitarianism.

This case of R v Jogee is the best example of this situation that liberty is not immoral for lack of self-discipline, disrespectful to people or life, indulge. Fyfe murdered by Jogee & Hirshi. Lack of self-discipline found on the part of Jogee & Hirshi who also became disrespectful to Fyfe, but it cannot be said that the theory indulge them. UKSC punished both them, but with right punishment for the right offence. When Jogee had no intention to murder Fyfe, them punishing and holding him guilty for murder would be over punishment. This was done in Powell & English's case that the prosecution failed to identify the proper witness of different parties which does not mean that theory is indulging the wrong. It is all about how one is able to interpret situation in light of the theories.

Conclusion:-

We can conclude by saying that equality and freedom, if not granted in any society, then the laws of that society need be changed to uphold the liberty of everyone because liberty uphold the value of human beings as human being which is essential for the development of any healthy society.

References:-

- *https://treasuryofenglishlaws.wordpress.com/2019/04/10/liberalism-the-law/*

<u>Anything to note?</u>

Rule of Recognition

by H.L.A. Hart

Issue:-

The internal point of view theory is not at all inadequate if it is backed by the theory of external point of view. The theory of rule of recognition provided by professor Hart neither underestimate nor refuse to accept the disagreement between officials of legal system. The theory of rule of recognition developed as a solution of this problem.

Case Study: R v Jogee & R v Ruddock:-

ISSUE:- The question of law was whether the common law took a wrong turning in two cases, Chan Wing-Siu v The Queen and Regina v Powell and English.

FACTS:- The appellant Jogee was convicted at Nottingham Crown Court of the murder of Paul Fyfe. Mr Fyfe was the boyfriend of Naomi Reid and he was stabbed to death in the hallway of her home in the early hours of 10 June 2011 by the appellant's co-defendant, Mohammed Hirsi. Hirsi was convicted of murder. The appellant and Hirsi spent the previous evening at various places, taking drink and drugs. They became increasingly intoxicated and increasingly aggressive. Shortly before midnight they arrived at Ms Reid's house. She told them to leave and They left but Hirsi returned and was there when Mr Fyfe arrived. Hirsi entered the house and there was an angry confrontation between him and Mr Fyfe. The appellant was outside with a bottle and shouting to Hirsi to do something to Mr Fyfe and at one stage the appellant came to the door and threatened to smash the bottle over Mr Fyfe's head. The fatal stabbing was done by Hirsi with a knife which he took from the kitchen. The judge directed the jury that the appellant was guilty of murder if he took part in the attack on Mr Fyfe and realised that it was possible that Hirsi might use the knife with intent to cause serious harm. The appellant Ruddock was convicted in the Circuit Court at

Montego Bay, Jamaica, of the murder of Peter Robinson. The appellant's co-defendant, Hudson, pleaded guilty to the murder. Mr Robinson was a taxi driver and the prosecution's case was that the murder was committed in the course of robbing him of his station wagon. The police evidence was that the appellant made a statement under caution which amounted to an admission that he was involved in committing the robbery and that he was present when Hudson killed the victim by cutting his throat but a denial that the appellant was responsible for the killing. The judge directed the jury that Ruddock was guilty of murder if he took part in the robbery and knew that there was a possibility that Hudson might intend to kill the victim.

JUDGMENT:- The unanimous conclusion of the court is that Chan Wing-Siu and Powell and English did take a wrong turning and these appeals should therefore be allowed. The correct rule is that foresight is simply evidence, albeit sometimes strong evidence, of intent to assist or encourage, which is the proper mental element for establishing secondary liability.

Is Internal point of view really Inadequate:-

Rule of recognition speaks about Semantic Sting which says that there no adequate account of law can be based on a description solely of how people speak. Rule of Recognition discuss mostly what law is or what supreme criterion dominates over the rest along with the Ultimate Rule of Austin which deals with tacit consent of theory. Rule of recognition means a rule must be recognized from both *internal point of view* means from acceptance of social practice which is not unproblematic and from the perspective of *external point of view* which means firstly, why anyone would accept the rule of recognition and secondly, no acceptance of social practice without questioning it. This external point of view can be named as Power-conferring rules. Power-conferring rules are Secondary rules which has some special characteristics, firstly, there are the rules of change that introduce private and public powers of legislation and repeal and 'cure' the defect of lack of progress. Secondly, it introduces the rules of adjudication and these 'cure' the defect of inefficiency by introducing the courts and other institutions of law enforcement. Finally, there is the rule of recognition which, by conferring power on people to identify the law for certain through the institution of criteria of legal validity, 'cures' the 'defect' of uncertainty. This secondary rules deals with the doctrine of Penumbra. The doctrine of Penumbra deals to remove uncertainty from laws about what the law requires. Rule of recognition is inadequate without secondary rules, but not otherwise.

Here in this case, the internal point view or the social practice was that that bringing harm or injury to another is illegal, if done either individually or jointly. This is an unproblematic view, but problem starts with external point of view that when the principal & accessory had different intention & no knowledge that the principal is going to harm & injure Fyfe by knife, then why anyone would accept that rule of recognition and secondly Jogee challenged this question because there is no acceptance of social practice without questioning it. There was a gray are about the liability of secondary part which defect or penumbra had been removed by rules of adjudication because UKSC decided that Jogee had no intention or knowledge to harm or injure Fyfe with knife, so he cannot be guilty of that crime on what his principal thought about & not him. He must be liable for the right offence means manslaughter.

Rule of Recognition underestimate the existence & disagreement between officials of legal system:-

Rule-Following means habitual Obedience form the internal point of view which is a concept laid down jurist Austin as OBT or Order Backed by Threats is an Idea of Internal point of view. Paradox of Rule-Following says that when we are playing chess, there are some rules of Chess we have to follow. Also there are new interpretations of rule which we can use while playing chess. Inspired from this chess rule professor Hart developed the Linguistic Method or Linguistic Philosophy which has two wings:

- Firstly, Primary rules mean subjects are being obliged to be forced from sovereign power which also imposes duty.

- Secondly, Secondary rules means subjects are being under an obligation. This deals with morality or what law ought to be. This is an Idea of Obligation which can remove pre-legal or social defects in cases of static, inefficient, uncertain.

For example, in this case, the problem lies with interpretation of liability of secondary party. Powell & English's stood a wrong turn, but Jogee & Ruddcok's case corrected that difficulty by removing the static, inefficient, uncertain defects of social practice. If the rule of recognition underestimates the existence and disagreement between officials of legal system, then it would not be able to produce the Linguistic method which is extremely helpful to prevent disagreements between officials of legal system.

Criticism by Finnis:-

Finnis says that the natural law is that the central set of elements constituting an official's acceptance of a rule of recognition, is a moral acceptance of the rule. According to Fuller, rule of recognition of natural law by officials are treated as moral acceptance of the rule. So, fuller is accepting the rule of positivism indirectly. Natural laws when recognized by officials then that become positive laws and Fuller is accepting that as moral acceptance of the rule. As defences against Natural Law & Fuller's criticism Hart says that his theory of legal realism is based on nature of legal reasoning. It says about the difference between what law is & how it expressed. It also says that positivist are formalising & ignoring the facts of adjudication & judicial law making. Penumbral cases are required to settle the meaning of legal rules. Indeed, natural law is the central acceptance of rule of recognition because there was no usual manual provided by nature to us except our cognitive thinking. Past decades, rulers decide cases by depending upon morality and that precedent treated as positive law. Here we cannot say that Finnis said anything wrong.

In this case, a gray area was there at the statutes & the previous precedents too. UKSC judges decided that what is morally right in this situation. This case is a fit evidence to show that what Hart says that there is a difference between what is law & how it expressed is true absolutely. The law says that Jogee & Hirshi are both liable to bring harm & injury to Fyfe, but how much which need proper interpretation where Finnis's natural law entries. Depending on morality, UKSC said that Jogee cannot be held liable for murder which is committed by his principle & not him because he had neither any knowledge nor intention. So, in this criticism we can say that both Finnis & hart are right from their own perspectives.

Criticism by Dworkin:-

Dworkin identified the rule of recgonition as a matter of empirical fact which is to cure the defect of uncertainty in a society of primary rules alone. Here, Dworkin rightly said this because primary rules can be tested by secondary rules. According to Dworkin three things follow from this:

First Point:- The judge has to act as a legislator to make new law for the future on whether rollerskates are prohibited or not, and this is contrary to what we suppose the judicial role to be or judges are not elected to legislate. Here, we cannot agree 100% with Dworkin because Judges are the experts. Historically, everywhere experts are generally selected and elected. If election starts here, then that has to be granted by primary rules. Primary rules are made by legislators and can be use for their benefit at any time. Primary rules are OBT which can cause injustice to people by using threat of force because it lays the foundation of dictatorship. This can only be removed by testing primary rules through secondary rules which is decided by judges and that is a form of democracy. So, we need experts and independence of those experts, otherwise sovereign power compel them to bring injustice for their own benefit which can give raise to an unhealthy society and civil war.

For example, in this case, Parliament is elected, but they left a gray area in statute that about liability of secondary party in accordance with his/her involved intention to the crime of complicity. Jogee assisted & encouraged, but not to bring injury or harm to Fyfe through knife. Here we need an expert like judiciary. Judges of UKSC solved this puzzle playing the role of judicial legislation. Unless they acted in this manner, this penumbra would never get clarity.

Second Point:- Dworkin said firstly that the judge characteristically then applies that law to the defendant, and so this would be retrospective legislation, which is unfair and not how we think judges act. Retrospective legislation is not unfair at all. History says that when if there is no law no-one can be punished and how can we identify that we need a law here? That can only be decided by using retrospective legislation. Human beings can imagine, but not every situation. At 1215, no-one imagined about cyber crime, but in 21st century when cyber crime started, then we feel that we need a law here. So, retrospective legislation is not unfair. Secondly, Dworkin is differing in his own statement. If judges characteristically apply the laws, then why he provided the theory of pre-interpretation where no values are attached to the rules which can be challenged by interpretation stage and finally laws can be changed at post-interpretative stage. If judges apply laws characteristically, then at post-interpretative stage it cannot be changed as Dworkin said.

For Example, in this case, there was no scope to imagine that one can attack in Fyfe's house & Fyfe is going to die at that night. Jogee & Hirshi did the crime & then we got the circumstances to decide what is right & what is wrong which is called retrospectivity. This is not bad at all.

Third Point:- Judges must continually be misdescribing what they are doing, because they talk as if they were finding the law, rather than legislating. Judges are not misdescribing their work at all. Sometimes they interpret laws where factual moral disagreement in question and sometime make laws like legislatures where they find that the existence of that law is *ultra-vires* or the non-existence of that can bring frustration that human life is not good which can stand in the way of welfare society.

For example, considering this case, we can find that Powell & English's case was misdescribed the principle of liability of secondary party, but UKSC overruled that by deciding the correct liability of secondary party in Jogee's case. Human being can always do mistakes, but our English legal system has the capacity to correct its mistakes.

Criticism by Fuller by 8 Inner Morality:-

Be promulgated:- Here, Hart prevails over Fuller. Promulgation means whether the law is in action by getting its force or not. If the law does not get its force automatically from the date it is getting royal assent, then whether that law has been promulgated or got its force in law, has to be tested by secondary rules because promulgation is related to primary rules. In this case we can find that the laws of secondary liability are always is in force and it's been tested in a series of cases like Powell, English, Jogee, Ruddock & so on.

Not be retroactive:- There is no question arises that every laws must be retrospective. Again, Hart prevails over Fuller. If laws are retroactive, then that can bring injustice because human being can think, but cannot think much further for future. For example, this case evident that no-one could anyone imagined that on that night Fyfe is going to be dead by Jogee & Hirshi with one of their separate intentions. So, neither Fuller suggested that any particular law is retroactive, nor any question of retroactivity arises here.

Be general:- Again, Hart prevails over Fuller because whether primary rules are creating any discrimination or not, that has to be tested by secondary rules. In this case, the laws relating to intention of secondary party has been decided & that is applicable generally with no discrimination except if the defendant has any defence on his or her side.

Be clear:- Again, Hart prevails over Fuller. Penumbra cases must be decided and the gaps must be filled by judicial legislation. There was a gray about intention of secondary party which UKSC decided & brought clarity to the law that Jogee must be punished for manslaughter & not for murder.

Not be inconsistent:- Again, Hart prevails over Fuller because whether any primary rule is inconsistent or _ultra vires_ or not that also has to be decided by judicial legislation of secondary rules. In this case, laws were inconstant because Powell & English were inconstant with principles laid down at Woolmington v DPP which has been removed by UKSC in the case of Jogee & Ruddock.

Not require the impossible:- Again, Hart prevails over Fuller because if the primary rules are impossible to be achieved, only that can be set aside or declared _ultra vires_ by secondary rule of recognition. In this case, nothing is impossible we can find. Intention of the accessory must be found out which must clearly match with his or her principal.

Be 'congruent' or consistent with official action:- Again, Hart prevails over Fuller because whether the law consistent or not has to tested by secondary rules of recognition. This judgment of R v Jogee & Ruddock bring clarity to the provisions of the statue about intention of secondary party.

Be reasonably stable that is, not change too frequently:- Again, Hart prevails over Fuller because if the changes regularly, then definitely people will do mistakes. To cure those mistakes, we need secondary rules and also to bring stability to legislation, we need secondary rules of recognition as ultimate check. The laws of secondary liability were stable even though it took wrong turning. This case of R v Jogee will bring long stability because this principle settled the by bringing clarity to it.

Conclusion:-

We can conclude by saying that rule of recognition is inadequate without secondary rules and it in certain ways can underestimate the existence and disagreement between legal officials to solve which it took birth.

Reference:-

- https://treasuryofenglishlaws.wordpress.com/2019/04/10/harts-rule-of-recognition/

<u>Anything to note?</u>

Hard v Soft Positivism

Issue:-

The issue relating to this case is whether Dworkin was able to provide an efficient mechanism which can be used to find out morality where the law is uncertain or not. Indeed, he picked up from there where Judge Harcules, Professor Hart or Raz left off. It is extremely advantageous to use soft positivism, but depending upon the nature of the deciding authority. The case of R vJogee & Ruddock is the perfect one to define the theories of Dworkin because this is a hard case.

Case Study: R v Jogee & R v Ruddock:-

ISSUE:- The question of law was whether the common law took a wrong turning in two cases, Chan Wing-Siu v The Queen and Regina v Powell and English.

FACTS:- The appellant Jogee was convicted at Nottingham Crown Court of the murder of Paul Fyfe. Mr Fyfe was the boyfriend of Naomi Reid and he was stabbed to death in the hallway of her home in the early hours of 10 June 2011 by the appellant's co-defendant, Mohammed Hirsi. Hirsi was convicted of murder. The appellant and Hirsi spent the previous evening at various places, taking drink and drugs. They became increasingly intoxicated and increasingly aggressive. Shortly before midnight they arrived at Ms Reid's house. She told them to leave and They left but Hirsi returned and was there when Mr Fyfe arrived. Hirsi entered the house and there was an angry confrontation between him and Mr Fyfe. The appellant was outside with a bottle and shouting to Hirsi to do something to Mr Fyfe and at one stage the appellant came to the door and threatened to smash the bottle over Mr Fyfe's head. The fatal stabbing was done by Hirsi with a knife which he took from the kitchen. The judge directed the jury that the appellant was guilty of murder if he took part in the attack on Mr Fyfe and realised that it was possible that Hirsi might use the knife with intent to cause serious harm. The appellant Ruddock was convicted in the Circuit Court at Montego Bay, Jamaica, of the murder of Peter Robinson. The appellant's co-defendant, Hudson, pleaded guilty to the murder. Mr Robinson was a taxi driver and the prosecution's case was that the murder was committed in the course of robbing him of his station wagon. The police evidence was that the appellant made a statement under caution which amounted to an admission that he was involved in committing the robbery and that he was present when Hudson killed the victim by cutting his throat but a denial that the appellant was responsible for the killing. The judge directed the jury that Ruddock was guilty of murder if he took part in the robbery and knew that there was a possibility that Hudson might intend to kill the victim.

JUDGMENT:- The unanimous conclusion of the court is that Chan Wing-Siu and Powell and English did take a wrong turning and these appeals should therefore be allowed. The correct rule is that foresight is simply evidence, albeit sometimes strong evidence, of intent to assist or encourage, which is the proper mental element for establishing secondary liability.

Dworkin's Theory to Address Problems of Hard Positivism:-

Dworkin's theory of law-as-interpretation picks up where legal positivism left off. *Hard conventionalism* means no to derive from the words of the law. *Soft positivism or conventionalism* means firstly, that judges should decide cases in the manner that judges should decide cases and secondly, there has to be a convention among judges that this the way they should decide cases. According to dworkin there are generally four stages, namely, semantic stage, jurisprudential stage, doctrinal stage, adjudicative stage. Dworkin's theory of interpretation divides the soft conventionalism or semantic stage of interpretation into three stages, as follows:

- *Pre-interpretative* means where no attitude is stuck towards the value of the rule.
- *Interpretative* means questioning, differing, doing-argument against the long established principles.
- *Post-Interpretation* means the principle has fold back into it and it has an effect of changing the original rule.

Law is the rule of life and the mentality of people cannot be changed unless the change can be brought into their stereotypic mentality. When that is not possible by general awareness, then that must be bringing through legal institutions to maintain a healthy and welfare society. It is true that it is impossible to do any enactment, stating all upcoming problems there. So, limitations are there because of uncertainty which can bring rigidity to the law and society. Dworkin's theory of interpretation solved this problem of rigidity.

Here, in this case, we can find that statutes are there, but those statutes are not clearly defining about when knowledge & intention differs then what liability the secondary party have. So, *hard positivism* cannot be applied here. So, we have to focus on soft positivism. At pre-interpretative stage Powell, English & other previous cases decided that accessory must be guilty for the same offence as his or her principal does. At interpretative stage, this was challenged by R v Jogee & Ruddock's case and at Post-Interpretative stage the principle has fold back into it and it has an effect of changing the original rule that accessory & principal requires same amount of knowledge & intention to be liable for same amount of charges. If that intention or knowable varies, then accessory & principal will be never charged for same offence.

Judicial Discretion In Terms of Adjudication:-

As Professor Hart says that Interpretive account of law includes the explicit settled law identified by reference to its social sources along with implicit legal principles which are those principles that both best fit or cohere with the explicit law and also provide the best moral justification for it. On this interpretive view, the law is never incomplete or indeterminate, so the judge never has occasion to step outside the law and exercise a law-creating power in order to reach a decision. Discretion is therefore for such implicit principles, with their moral dimensions, that courts should turn in those hard cases where the social sources of the law fail to determine a decision on some point of law. Constructive interpretation which is so prominent a feature of Dworkin's theory of adjudication, but though this procedure certainly defers, it does not eliminate the moment for judicial law-making, since in any hard case different principles supporting competing analogies may present themselves and a judge will often have to choose between them, relying, like a conscientious legislator, on his sense of what is best and not on any already established order of priorities prescribed for him by law. Judges should be entrusted with law-making powers to deal with disputes which the law fails to regulate may be regarded as a necessary price to pay for avoiding the inconvenience of alternative methods of regulating them such as reference to the legislature. If there is any gray area left and unless discretion as judicial legislation cannot be exercised, then there will be a dictatorship and rules made by legislature and other legislating bodies will go unchecked.

For example, in this case, we can find that this is a very hard case because the sources were took a wrong turn while interpreting them. There were no best fit laws in this issue. So, in the case of Jogee & Ruddock, the court must decide the liability of secondary party according to its intention & knowledge of the crime to determine the best fit or cohere with the explicit law and also provide the best moral justification for it, as identified by professor Hart. Judges are entrusted here with their law-making power to find out the proper liability of secondary party because statutes failed to describe that clearly & previous precedents took a wrong turning. Unless judges have this power, then injustice will spread on that society & again people will went on to civil war, after a long suffering.

Dworkin Grants Judges the Greatest Amount of Discretion in Hard Cases:-

Dworkin's other criticism of judicial discretion condemns it not as descriptively false but for endorsing a form of law-making which is undemocratic and unjust. Judges are not usually elected and in a democracy. So, only the elected representatives of the people should have law-making powers. Dworkin makes the further accusation that judicial lawmaking is unjust and condemns it as a form of retrospective or ex post facto law-making which is, of course, commonly regarded as unjust, but the reason for regarding retrospective law-making as unjust is that it disappoints the justified expectations of those who, in acting, have relied on the assumption that the legal consequences of their acts will be determined by the known state of the law established at the time of their acts. Dworkin says that judges should not depart from the principle where the law is settled, but where there is gray area or uncertainty has been found, there discretion should be used as mechanical measure to meet that fill-up the gap for the welfare of the society. It is true that disagreed that Dworkin granted the greatest amount of discretion. It is also true that judges are unelected, but they are expert in this field. When Parliament or executive encroaches upon the rights of common people, then these unelected judges are the only one who could save the society from unholy whims. Selection is always different than election. Selection is always for experts and without experts there cannot be survival of society. If doctor can save people's life by using their discretionary power achieved through their skills, then judges are also can save the society by using their discretionary power achieved through their skills, may be have unlimited power from it.

This case evident that, maybe judges are not elected, we need their judicial law-making power because they are experts and experts are selected & not elected. Parliament is elected, but the statute it passed does not clearly defined that if intention & knowledge differ while committing any crime between accessory & principal, then what the liability or the charges one must bring against the accessory. For this reason Powell, English or other previous case took wrong turning. We don't have any problem with elected Parliament, but if judiciary stops law making then who will suffer? The common people of our society which will increase frustration & can never bring peace through this kind of injustice. R v Jogee & Ruddock bring justice to secondary liability. Criminals also have rights. Maybe accessories are criminals & they did something wrong or performed some prohibited act, but they are also human being. Charging them for higher offence would violate their human rights too. This does not mean that they must go unpunished, but must be punished the appropriate crime.

Dworkin Used the Image of Hercules as Misleading:-

Judge Hercules said that interpretation of law is restricted to some certain kind of already defined interpretations with which Dworkin disagreed. In-fact, Dworkin is neither wrong here nor he used the image of Hercules misleading. Judge Hercules is also correct from his perspective, but he failed to think about unsettled problems which are developing for new developments.

For example, in this case, was the correct interpretation settled? No, that's the reason why UKSC went on find out the liability of accessories in a joint enterprise crime. Judge Hercules failed to view this point while criticising Dworkin. Here, Dworkin is absolutely right that judges should not act as legislator in every case, but where the meaning requires clarity, then they must step aside from it.

Dworkin's Mistaken View:-

Critics says that Dworkin has a mistaken view that there is always right to answer legal problems and when a right answer is available then that answer is moral. As peter Devlin says that it depends on the mentality of judges who are using the discretion with which I cannot disagree.

For example, in this case, we find that Powell, English & all other previous precedents were treated as right before the pronouncement of judgment of R v Jogee & Ruddock. So, definitely, as professor Devlin said, it depends upon the mentality of judges. Also, there must be an answer to every legal problem & the right answer must contain morality. In this case we can find that Jogee & Hirshi went to bring harm or injury to Fyfe. Until this their intentions were common, but Jogee encouraged to smash the bottle over Fyfe's head & Hirshi stabbed Fyfe with knife. Here, we don't the mentality of Jogee that if he knew that Hirshi is going to stab Fyfe with knife, then whether he supported him or not. So, from this point knowledge & intention differed. So, after many challenges like Powell, English and other previous cases, finally, the question of law challenged before UKSC through R v Jogee & Ruddock was able to the right answer which contains morality.

Judges Ought to Decide through Principles:-

Dworkin's difference between principles and policies says that judges ought to decide case by principles and not policies. Dworkin did not mean that. Policy means community goals and principle mean tested rules. Judges are often have to test different policies to give relief to common people. They have to use principles means the rules which are already tested and established to test that policy. If anyone wants to derive from this conception, then there is no harm to depart from it, if that is not harmful for the society because Dworkin used the word "ought" here. Ought cannot be treated as must or is. Secondly, some critics say that Dworkin's theory is based on inadequate and misleading distinctions:

- Firstly, between rules and principles; &

- Secondly, between principles and policies which is also not true at all. Rules are general and tested or untested laws. Principles are established laws through tested rules and finally, policies are community goals. His distinction between rules, principles and policies are extremely clear and there is nothing unclear.

For example, here in this case, we can find that Parliament to achieve the best community goals set up the laws of joint enterprise which have some gray area. Courts are not creating community goals which we call policies, rather it deal specific problem like Powell, English, Jogee, Ruddock & other cases to bring clarity to those policies. All these cases means Powell, English were laid down some principles which requires to be tested. So, judges decide cases sometimes depending upon policies when there no uncertainty and sometimes through principles when there is no principal exist on that matter or has any gray area.

Dworkin & Riggs v Palmer:-

Dworkin addresses this by introducing the principle of salience: If a significant number of states, encompassing a significant population, has developed an agreed code of practice, either by treaty or by other form of coordination, then other states have at least a prima facie duty to subscribe to that practice as well, with the important proviso that this duty holds only if a more general practice to that effect, expanded in that way, would improve the legitimacy of the subscribing state and the international order as a whole. The 'principle of mitigation' compels sovereign states to adjust their practices, when these are shown to fall short of standards of moral rightness. Dworkin addresses this by introducing the principle of salience: If a significant number of states, encompassing a significant population, has developed an agreed code of practice, either by treaty or by other form of coordination, then other states have at least a prima facie duty to subscribe to that practice as well, with the important proviso that this duty holds only if a more general practice to that effect, expanded in that way, would improve the legitimacy of the subscribing state and the international order as a whole. The 'principle of mitigation' compels sovereign states to adjust their practices, when these are shown to fall short of standards of moral rightness. This will gradually lead to a cosmopolitan moral and legal integration.

Here, in this case, Principles of silence or Principles of mitigation has no application because the highest court of United Kingdom, the UKSC, decided the case & remove the gap successfully. Where highest court fails to do so, there individual can bring claim internationally which is concern about this case.

McLoughlin v O'Brian:-

In Dworkin's view, substantive arguments are relating to the people's right to be treated as equals, have to be selected to fit means the already existing case law. Mrs McLoughlin learned that her husband and children were involved in a car accident. She set out for the hospital some miles away, and when she got there she was told her daughter was dead and she saw that her husband and other children were seriously injured. She suffered severe shock and she sued, among others, the driver of the vehicle, whose negligence caused the accident. Dworkin says that Judge Hercules might begin by considering the following six possible interpretations of the case law:

- Success for the plaintiff only where there is physical injury. We can rule this out immediately because it does not fit the law of tort. It is clear from the case law that damages may be obtained for nervous shock. Here, I am disagreeing with Dworkin because mind & body are not different.we feel pain at our forebrain. So, psychological injury is not different than physical injury.

- Success only where the emotional injury occurs at the accident, not later. Dworkin says that this would just draw a morally arbitrary line. 'Morally arbitrary line': here Dworkin is attacking the idea that there is law plus moral principle. He thinks finding out what the law is, as opposed to what it ought to be, includes the relevant principle. Indeed, she did not suffered pain later on because the death of her child happed in front of her eyes at hospital.

- Success only where a practice of awarding someone like Mrs McLoughlin would be economically efficient. This, Dworkin says, is a matter of government policy, and so is irrelevant to the question of the plaintiff's rights. Money can never compensate the life Mr. MacLoughlin & her child, but it is required to help her on those days when she is in trauma & require it for several purposes. For example, her psychological treatment, paying hospitals bills, women often take break at their career for their family life, so to buy things of livelihood & so on.

- Success only where the injury, whether physical or emotional, is the direct consequence of the accident. He rules out this interpretation because it is 'contrary to fit', contradicting the clear case law, where there is a test of foreseeability which limits the liability of the person who causes the accident. Can foreseeability pay relief to Mrs McLoughlin? No because it was not her fault. She was not present at the moment in that car. So, I am unable to agree with Dworkin.

- Success only where the injury is foreseeable by the defendants. Again, how can foreseeability pay relief to Mrs McLoughlin, when she was not present when the accident took place? It was not her fault. She was not present at the moment in that car. So, I am unable to agree with Dworkin.

- Success for foreseeable injury, except where an unfair financial burden is placed on the person who causes the accident. By 'unfair', Dworkin means that the compensation would be disproportionately large compared with the moral blame in causing the accident. Losing her own child or suffering of husband means her loved ones can never cause disproportionate large compensation comparing with the moral blame because no amount of money can compensate the loss of life of child & suffering of husband.

According to Dworkin, 5 and 6 are the best contenders. To develop the analysis further: 1 and 4 are ruled out because they contradict the requirement of 'fit'. The claim that psychological trauma is not recoverable in a negligence action simply contradicts the line of decisions. Thus the claim does not 'fit' the law. The same goes for the claim that Mrs McLoughlin cannot succeed because her injury was 'indirectly' caused, since it is clear that many actions in negligence have succeeded where the injury was indirectly caused (most nervous shock cases, in fact). 2 is ruled out because it is an interpretation that relies on an arbitrary assertion that only people at the scene can recover. It is 'morally irrelevant' to draw a distinction between what happened in the case and the same scenario occurring at the scene of the accident, since this was obviously in the 'aftermath' of the accident (as the Court of Appeal said) and, of course, it was not as if Mrs McLoughlin was a stranger to the victims. 3 is ruled out because it relies on policy, not principle.

Here, in this case also we find a situation like this that Fyfe's girl-friend was present at that time when Jogee & Hirshi were stabbed Fyfe to death, but does it mean that Jogee needs to be punished for higher offence which he had not done. Compensation cannot compensate the life of loved ones, but if accessory has been punished for the same amount crime done by his principal, then that neither can bring justice to Fyfe's girlfriend nor it can bring reformation Jogee which is the main aim of punishment.

Conclusion:-

We can conclude by saying that Dworkin's theory of interpretation of law not only solved the problem where hard positivism left off, but also uphold the right of democracy for the well-being and better future of any society.

References:-

- https://treasuryofenglishlaws.wordpress.com/2019/04/24/hard-v-soft-positivism/

Anything to note?

Natural Law & Rights

Issue:-

There is no shortcoming in the theories of Aquinas and Finnis which can be found on their theory of naturalistic conception of morality and law. The natural tradition has never suffered from any misunderstanding, but it reject unjust law is no law when any issue in question. The two types of natural law theories provided by Finnis and Fuller are in complexity when they do injustice.

Case Study: R v Jogee & R v Ruddock:-

ISSUE:- The question of law was whether the common law took a wrong turning in two cases, Chan Wing-Siu v The Queen and Regina v Powell and English.

FACTS:- The appellant Jogee was convicted at Nottingham Crown Court of the murder of Paul Fyfe. Mr Fyfe was the boyfriend of Naomi Reid and he was stabbed to death in the hallway of her home in the early hours of 10 June 2011 by the appellant's co-defendant, Mohammed Hirsi. Hirsi was convicted of murder. The appellant and Hirsi spent the previous evening at various places, taking drink and drugs. They became increasingly intoxicated and increasingly aggressive. Shortly before midnight they arrived at Ms Reid's house. She told them to leave and They left but Hirsi returned and was there when Mr Fyfe arrived. Hirsi entered the house and there was an angry confrontation between him and Mr Fyfe. The appellant was outside with a bottle and shouting to Hirsi to do something to Mr Fyfe and at one stage the appellant came to the door and threatened to smash the bottle over Mr Fyfe's head. The fatal stabbing was done by Hirsi with a knife which he took from the kitchen. The judge directed the jury that the appellant was guilty of murder if he took part in the attack on Mr Fyfe and realised that it was possible that Hirsi might use the knife with intent to cause serious harm. The appellant Ruddock was convicted in the Circuit Court at

Montego Bay, Jamaica, of the murder of Peter Robinson. The appellant's co-defendant, Hudson, pleaded guilty to the murder. Mr Robinson was a taxi driver and the prosecution's case was that the murder was committed in the course of robbing him of his station wagon. The police evidence was that the appellant made a statement under caution which amounted to an admission that he was involved in committing the robbery and that he was present when Hudson killed the victim by cutting his throat but a denial that the appellant was responsible for the killing. The judge directed the jury that Ruddock was guilty of murder if he took part in the robbery and knew that there was a possibility that Hudson might intend to kill the victim.

JUDGMENT:- The unanimous conclusion of the court is that Chan Wing-Siu and Powell and English did take a wrong turning and these appeals should therefore be allowed. The correct rule is that foresight is simply evidence, albeit sometimes strong evidence, of intent to assist or encourage, which is the proper mental element for establishing secondary liability.

Classical Natural Lawyers Failed to Value Political Order & Stability:-

Historically, ancient Greeks from 16-17th centuries started to think that legal theory means law is the practical application of morality. It begins with Plato, Aristotle, Scotics and they described it as how ought a man to live. Plato was concerned about Justice & other absolute values of justice. Justice brings morality to the values of political order & stability. So, we cannot say that Plato failed to recognize the value of political order & stability. Aristotle said that to understand man's telos means goals or purpose that reject his nature. Thomas Aquinas reconstructed from Greek to Rome to Christian teleology by his work that law is the Grace of God and not to conflict or abolish man's nature. It was modified Aristotle that man's end is not only to live socially & seek knowledge, but also to live in a Christian community. Here, it is evident that Thomas Aquinas failed to recognize the natural theory of law. There are many religions we have in our world. Morality deals with freedom & liberty. Professing religion must be free in any society. If people are compelled to live in Christian community without their will & wish, then that is immoral. So, Aristotle was open minded, but Thomas Aquinas failed to recognise the value of political order & stability a little. Scotics said by reason man could determine rights that transcended in particular culture & therefore universally applicable. This is a very complex issue to be determined because when man determines rights which are particular to any culture, if that is moral then that brings value to political order & stability, but if that is immoral, then that law can overturn the political order & stability.

For example, in the cases of Powell of English, the prosecution failed to prove the case & the court punished accessory same as the principal. This is morally wrong which can bring trouble to political order & stability, but in the case of Jogee & Ruddock when the issue of liability of secondary party has been determined in accordance with morality in law, then that can never overturn the political order & stability. Natural lawyers always speak about law with morality. So, it cannot be said that they failed to value the political order & stability.

Aquinas Failed to Naturalistic Conception of Morality & Law:-

Thomas Aquinas reconstructed from Greek to Rome to Christian teleology by his work that law is the Grace of God and not to conflict or abolish man's nature. It was modified Aristotle that man's end is not only to live socially & seek knowledge, but also to live in a Christian community. Here, it is evident that Thomas Aquinas failed to recognize the natural theory of law. There are many religions we have in our world. Morality deals with freedom & liberty. Professing religion must be free in any society. If people are compelled to live in Christian community without their will & wish, then that is immoral. Here, we can say that Aquinas failed in theory of natural laws & natural rights to view the proper conception of morality and law. Moreover, Thomas Aquinas defined two sources of law. Firstly, Specifio means specified or laws laid down or deduced from natural law and secondly, Determinatio means determination or man decided which is compatible with natural law which is not different than each other. This theory also proves that Aquinas failed to view naturalistic conception of morality & law properly, because we derived morality from our cognitive development. Cognitive development always speaks about guilty mind differentiating between what is right and what is wrong. When morality or the natural laws are codified in statute then that is called positive laws. When positive laws are tested & pronounced in judgments that Aquinas is describing as determination. Judges decide cases & fill-up gaps by using the doctrine of penumbra where there is any moral disagreement. So, Aquinas failed to describe the theory of naturalistic conception of law and morality properly. Again, He divided this orders of law into further four wings, as follows:

- Eternal Law means universe governed or divine law;
- Natural law means human reason & Free will;
- Human law means rules, regulations, using reason and deduced from natural law;
- Divine law which revealed God to men.

Before defining the case of Jogee & Roddock in light of this case, I want to highlight one point that firstly, eternal law are not different than divine law which has been revealed from God to men that is based on morality, secondly, Natural law which speaks about human reason & free will are developed on cognitive morality, finally, human laws means positive laws developed depending upon natural law because natural laws when written, it become positive law. So, eternal law or divine law or natural law or human made laws are not different each other.

Here, in this case, our guilty mind or morality says that bringing harm or injuries to others are wrong. Natural law says this and when it decided through the cases like Powell or English, then this principle became positive law for joint enterprise crimes which had some uncertainty in it and R v Jogee & Ruddock's case removed that uncertainty. So, we can say that Thomas Aquinas defined law severally, but he failed on to naturalistic conception of specifio & Determinatio because law is one like God means natural law which human decide & record through their cognitive skills.

Finnis Failed on to Naturalistic Conception of Morality & Law:-

Finnis considered one very important factor that cognitivists says that human must know moral values & principles to judge and what is just expressions of our emotional attitudes. The Cognitive Theory says that we derived morality from our cognitive development. Cognitive development always speaks about guilty mind differentiating between what is right and what is wrong. So, Finnis never failed to recognise the difference between emotion and reason and so he was able to recognise the naturalistic conception of morality & law.

In this case, we can find that the wrong turning made at Powell & English has been corrected by UKSC. UKSC identified the morality perfectly for the moral liability of secondary party. So, we can never say that Finnis failed on to naturalistic conception of morality & law.

Common Good & Positive Law by Finnis:-

John Finnis was a realist. The theory of good life was provided him because he drew a relation between common good and positive law. His theory of scepticism or realist describes that moral values & principles does exists in law. The requirement of morality deals with Fact means value distinction, description & prescription, factual & normative, describe some aspects of reality & evaluate that or prescribe behaviour. The famous theory of John Finnis's Natural Fallacy says that Natural rights are generally decided by what rights are ought to be. Finnis's theory is more relavent than before because it says that in the period of crisis, we need agreement on basic values that we do not allow the law to endanger. Law can never allowed be to be in endanger. Agreements are also a part of law. At the period of crisis, if the agreement of basic values are not made and continued with morality, then that brings danger for human beings. Then those immoral agreements must save human beings by application of laws because laws always uphold that what is morally and ethically correct for human survival.

Here, in this case, no crisis period can be found when Powell-English case has been decided, but it takes one moment to raise voice which can lead to a crisis period at any time. So, Jogee-Ruddock has been decided at perfect time which brought morality to law to save the society on any eventual crisis on this aspect.

Criticism by Hart:-

This theory of good life was criticized by H.L.A. Hart. Hart says that legal realism deals with nature of legal reasoning. There is a difference between what law is & how it expressed. Positivists are formalising & ignoring the facts of adjudication & judicial law making. Penumbral cases are required to settle the meaning of legal rules. Hart was very profound interest on the requirements of Procedural Justice. According to Hart procedural justice satisfies the demands of morality, important idea of fidelity to law, obedience with moral justification. On this aspect I am disagreeing with professor Hart because Finnis also said that what law is contains both the principle of positive & natural law because Positive law decide & record what natural law is saying depending upon morality. Secondly, how it expressed depends on the interpretation of human being which can lead to formation or worse of any crisis period.

In this case, the way Powell & English were decided was wrongly described about what the law is. Problem of interpretation can frustrate the whole procedure & lead to crisis where people start to protest for their rights to be protected, but in the case of Jogee, what the law is about the liability of secondary party has been defined clearly, depending upon both natural & positive laws. We cannot agree with professor Hart on his this criticism.

Misunderstanding about unjust laws are not laws:-

Critics claims that there is a principle that unjust laws are not laws, but sometimes that is not maintained by law. This is not true at all. The doctrine of Lex injusta non est lex means that an unjust law is not a law. Unjust means unjust according to the principal of morality or natural law. The natural Law originally means that it is a general moral theory that explains the nature of morality. Principally natural law describes theory of morality & not a theory of law. If there is a law which is immoral in nature, that can be set aside by judicial legislation.

For example, Powell & English was an unjust law which remains in force for a long time, but its defect has been removed by Jogee & Ruddock. So, a law may be unjust & remain in force for long decades, but that does not mean that the theory is wrong. Theory is there to support the wrong to correct. There is a misunderstanding that it is wrong to say that an unjust law is not law, but theory is correct which must not be misunderstood.

Complexity modern Natural Law theory:-

There are two types of theory, we can find in modern natural law theory. Firstly, Finnis's natural law theory which emphasis on content and secondly, Fuller's theory of inner morality which emphasis on the form. Fuller provided the most important theory of morality which deals with the rule of law. His theory of morally is very sound about aspects of governing by rules which give raise to a new theory which is the theory of Procedural Natural Law theory. This Procedural Natural Law theory deals with substantive law & to assess them with requirement of law-making and administration. Critics say that complexity of modern societies need the later and not the former which is not at all correct because these are interrelated. Fuller provided eight principles of inner morality:

- Be promulgated;
- Not be retroactive;
- Be general;
- Be clear;
- Not be inconsistent;
- Not require the impossible;
- Be 'congruent' or consistent with official action;
- Be reasonably stable that is, not change too frequently.

Law is a scheme of social justice & for welfare of society. If any law is not promulgated, or contains any deficiency because of its retroactive nature or not general do discriminations or not clear or consistent or unstable or impossible in nature, then this form of law can seek the help of content of law to be tested. Human beings made mistakes and if their cognitively has not been developed properly, then while seeking help of content natural law, if morality has not been identified correctly, that can frustrate the whole form of natural law. So, neither the content of natural law, nor the form of natural law can be taken lightly. Complexity can arise from any these forms.

For example, Powell & English's case was unclear and had deficiency about the clarity of liability of secondary party in joint liability crime. The laws decided in these two precedents were inconsistent with another precedent, named, Woolmington v DPP. This provision has been corrected in R v Jogee & Ruddock's case and now this law of liability for secondary party in a joint enterprise crime is complying all the criteria laid down by jurist Fuller to bring clarity to the theories of natural law.

Conclusion:-

We can conclude by saying that may be Thomas Aquinas failed to describe properly the naturalistic conception of natural laws, Finns never failed to so and the theory of modern natural rights argues that complexity can arise from form of natural laws, no matter it is the content or the form.

Reference:-

- *https://treasuryofenglishlaws.wordpress.com/2019/04/10/natural-law-rights/*

<u>Anything to note?</u>

Rule of Law by Lon Fuller

Issue:-

Lon Fuller not only provided an outline of requirements of rule of law, but also he provided two ambitious arguments that rule of law are necessary for law & morals. Professor H.L.A. Hart believes that laws are positive in nature which doesn't have morality in it which is contradicting with his own doctrine of penumbra cases. Raz believe that content of laws are based social facts and not morality which is not always true because immoral laws are either overrule the laws or overthrow the ruler. This case of R v Jogee & Ruddock proved, Hart & Raz's thinking of positive law that it does not have morality, wrong.

Case Study: R v Jogee & R v Ruddock:-

ISSUE:- The question of law was whether the common law took a wrong turning in two cases, Chan Wing-Siu v The Queen and Regina v Powell and English.

FACTS:- The appellant Jogee was convicted at Nottingham Crown Court of the murder of Paul Fyfe. Mr Fyfe was the boyfriend of Naomi Reid and he was stabbed to death in the hallway of her home in the early hours of 10 June 2011 by the appellant's co-defendant, Mohammed Hirsi. Hirsi was convicted of murder. The appellant and Hirsi spent the previous evening at various places, taking drink and drugs. They became increasingly intoxicated and increasingly aggressive. Shortly before midnight they arrived at Ms Reid's house. She told them to leave and They left but Hirsi returned and was there when Mr Fyfe arrived. Hirsi entered the house and there was an angry confrontation between him and Mr Fyfe. The appellant was outside with a bottle and shouting to Hirsi to do something to Mr Fyfe and at one stage the appellant came to the door and threatened to smash the bottle over Mr Fyfe's head. The fatal stabbing was done by Hirsi with a knife which he took from the kitchen. The judge directed the jury that the appellant was guilty of murder if he took part in the attack on Mr Fyfe and realised that it was possible that Hirsi might use the knife with intent to cause serious harm. The appellant Ruddock was convicted in the Circuit Court at Montego Bay, Jamaica, of the murder of Peter Robinson. The appellant's co-defendant, Hudson, pleaded guilty to the murder. Mr Robinson was a taxi driver and the prosecution's case was that the murder was committed in the course of robbing him of his station wagon. The police evidence was that the appellant made a statement under caution which amounted to an admission that he was involved in committing the robbery and that he was present when Hudson killed the victim by cutting his throat but a denial that the appellant was responsible for the killing. The judge directed the jury that Ruddock was guilty of murder if he took part in the robbery and knew that there was a possibility that Hudson might intend to kill the victim.

JUDGMENT:- The unanimous conclusion of the court is that Chan Wing-Siu and Powell and English did take a wrong turning and these appeals should therefore be allowed. The correct rule is that foresight is simply evidence, albeit sometimes strong evidence, of intent to assist or encourage, which is the proper mental element for establishing secondary liability.

Modern Natural Law:-

Rule of Laws are Procedural Standards. Fuller did not aim to produce a morality of law on the basis of a general moral theory in keeping with the ancient natural law traditions. He explained the moral content in the idea of 'the rule of law' means governance by rules and judicial institutions as opposed to other sorts of political decision-making or ordering. According to him, the morality is morality as 'legality' which means morally sound aspects of governing by rules. For this reason, Fuller is often credited with devising a 'procedural' natural law theory, in that he does not focus on the substantive content of legal rules and assess them as to whether they are moral or not, but rather concerns himself with the requirements of just law-making and administration.

Here, in this case, before Jogee's decision, there was a lacking in its of rule of law because the governance rules of secondary liability were governing by many statutes & precedents which challenged several times before different judicial institutions, but the rule did not contain any proper morality. No procedural natural law theory is included in this case, but there is a requirement of judicial law-making which is evident in this case that UKSC decided the requirement of intention to be liable same as principal for the accessory efficiently.

Rule of Law as Inner Morality of Law:-

The question of the connection between law and morality is not a simple one, and it is the most important in the Western philosophical tradition. The ideal of law is a system which citizens could obey. This is an ideal that remains a value or virtue against which to assess if the system is legal. The authority of law derives from a moral understanding between rules and that those are ruled. Citizens give moral respect to the Constitution which is legitimate and it is necessarily as a right and good thing. A total failure in any of these does not simply result in a bad system of law because this result in something that is not properly called a legal system at all. Law is a scheme of justice and there cannot be any law which is legal from the surface-level Legality, but contain full of large scale of violation of rule of law. If there is no morality, then that causes revolution & civil wars. Lon Fuller provided us eight principles of the 'inner morality' of law. This Inner morality of law includes:

- Be promulgated;
- Not be retroactive;
- Be general;
- Be clear;
- Not be inconsistent;

- Not require the impossible;
- Be congruent or consistent with official action;
- Be reasonably stable that is, not change too frequently.

The legal philosophy of Hart who was even though a positivist was always sensitive to the natural lawyer's claims, and again and again addressed the different connections he saw between morality and law. The work of Dworkin says that there is an intimate connection between morality and law. Dworkin believed that his theory refutes positivism, in part for its failure to account for the role moral theory plays when judges decide cases.

For example, Powell & English's case was unclear and had deficiency about the clarity of liability of secondary party in joint liability crime. The laws decided in these two precedents were inconsistent with another precedent, named, Woolmington v DPP. This provision has been corrected in R v Jogee & Ruddock's case and now this law of liability for secondary party in a joint enterprise crime is complying all the criteria laid down by jurist Fuller to bring clarity to the theories of natural law. Dworkin's view is correct here that in the case of Jogee & Ruddock, judicial legislation was necessary to remove the gray area.

Hart-Fuller debate:-

Hart says that there is no necessary connection between law and morality. A legal system can function effectively even though it is neither just nor moral whereas Fuller says that the instruments of arbitrary and tyrannical regimes are not properly called law. Hart and fuller agree that immoral and unjust legal systems are unlikely to be stable and long-lived with which we cannot disagree. Hart's Legal realism deals with the nature of legal reasoning. It speaks about the difference between what law is & how it is expressed. Positivism is not always bad. Natural laws are when written, it becomes positive laws and when there are any gray areas, judicial-legislation fills-up that. According to Hart, Positivist are formalising & ignoring the facts of adjudication and judicial law making because penumbral cases are have to be settle by meaning the meaning of legal rules. The requirements of Procedural Justice must satisfy the demands of morality, important idea of fidelity to law, obedience with moral justification.

Here, in this case, we can find that immorality of Powell & English's case about liability of secondary party has been removed by UKSC. As Hart & fuller says, it is evident from this case that immoral and unjust legal systems are unlikely to be stable and long-lived, but I cannot agree with Hart that there is no necessary connection between law & morality. If the connection was not necessary, then the liability of secondary party would never be settled by overruling Powell, English & other previous cases. The case of Jogee is based on legal reasoning which is based on morality. It is a misconception that Positivist are formalising & ignoring the facts of adjudication and judicial law and Hart's Legal realism deals with the nature of legal reasoning which speaks about the difference between what law is & how it is expressed depending upon morality because if the law is immoral, then that has to be overruled one day, as the case of Jogee corrected the meaning of secondary liability that same intention requires for accessory as principal to be guilty of the same crime as principal does. This precedent corrected the immorality of Powell, English & other previous cases.

The Sources of Thesis by Raz:-

The idea of Raz says that an adequate test for the existence and content of law must be based only on social facts, and not moral arguments with which I cannot agree because social facts are not based on immorality. People formed society to live safely, securely and to achieve happiness at the maximum sphere. If laws are immoral, then that brings injustice to society. Many times injustice happens because laws are immoral, but people challenged those laws and if the ruler is too rigid, then they move against those rules too. Laws cannot be based on immoral social facts. The idea of Raz is very similar to the Separability Thesis presented by professor Hart which means Law and morality is conceptually distinct. This also contradicts with his own view that if law and morality are conceptually distinct, then that is frustrating the idea of doctrine of penumbra which decides gray areas of laws.

This case of R v Jogee & Ruddock are great example of that. Social fact is that that binging harm or injury to others are wrongful acts. This has been crystallised in statues & judicial decisions that when 2 or more, having common intention, will bring harm or injury to others except having defences, then that act is wrongful & must be punished. This idea liability of secondary party brought immorality to the law which has been challenged through several litigations & finally in this case of Jogee this problem has been settled. So, the Separability Thesis is not correct in saying that law & morality is separate because if that is so, then in the case Jogee, UKSC would never decided that Powell, English & previous cases took wrong turning about the knowledge & intention of accessory which must be same as his/her principal.

Positivism v Natural Law:-

Human being are the product of evolution which synthesizes elements of geology, biology, chemistry, physics, and mathematics. Reasonableness denotes the presence of rational decision in human being. These rational decisions are taken through cognitive skills which in other works known as the theory of guilty mind. Positivism developed through guilty mind because when there is a claim, then that was decided by judges in ancient periods, depending upon morality or guilty mind which is natural law. After pronouncement of that judgment that became positive laws. Anti-Positivist says that Positivism doesn't include morality and without morality, there cannot be something good. Law can be morally problematic. It is true that there cannot be any good without morality or all problems are there because human being has moral feelings in them, but this cannot be agreed that positivism doesn't include morality. If any law does include morality, then that can be challenged and set aside by higher courts, depending upon the moral view of the judge concern.

Here, in this case, it is evident that the accessory & the principal's guilty mind were not present when they went to Fyfe's house. Fyfe need justice & our society needs protection from future attacks like this, but the statutes did not clarify about the degree of requirement of intention & knowledge of principal &

accessory which Jogee & Ruddock's can fixes. It is not always possible to maintain control on violence, but when people loses it, then institutions are there to correct it which does not mean that law has no morality in it.

Conclusion:-

We can conclude by saying that positive laws are neither different from Fuller's natural law theory nor it exclude morality from law.

References:-

- https://treasuryofenglishlaws.wordpress.com/2019/04/10/lon-fullers-rule-of-law/

<u>Anything to note?</u>

Authority of Law by Raz

Issue:-

Joseph Raz provided the theory of authority which speaks about hard positivism. His social thesis or the theory of separation says that content of law are not tested on morality. His paradox of authority says that every authority must be tested through with reasons which is against his view of social thesis.

Case Study: R v Jogee & R v Ruddock:-

ISSUE:- The question of law was whether the common law took a wrong turning in two cases, Chan Wing-Siu v The Queen and Regina v Powell and English.

FACTS:- The appellant Jogee was convicted at Nottingham Crown Court of the murder of Paul Fyfe. Mr Fyfe was the boyfriend of Naomi Reid and he was stabbed to death in the hallway of her home in the early hours of 10 June 2011 by the appellant's co-defendant, Mohammed Hirsi. Hirsi was convicted of murder. The appellant and Hirsi spent the previous evening at various places, taking drink and drugs. They became increasingly intoxicated and increasingly aggressive. Shortly before midnight they arrived at Ms Reid's house. She told them to leave and They left but Hirsi returned and was there when Mr Fyfe arrived. Hirsi entered the house and there was an angry confrontation between him and Mr Fyfe. The appellant was outside with a bottle and shouting to Hirsi to do something to Mr Fyfe and at one stage the appellant came to the door and threatened to smash the bottle over Mr Fyfe's head. The fatal stabbing was done by Hirsi with a knife which he took from the kitchen. The judge directed the jury that the appellant was guilty of murder if he took part in the attack on Mr Fyfe and realised that it was possible that Hirsi might use the knife with intent to cause serious harm. The appellant Ruddock was convicted in the Circuit Court at Montego Bay, Jamaica, of the murder of Peter Robinson. The appellant's co-defendant, Hudson, pleaded guilty to the murder. Mr Robinson was a taxi driver and the prosecution's case was that the murder was committed in the course of robbing him of his station wagon. The police evidence was that the appellant made a statement under caution which amounted to an admission that he was involved in committing the robbery and that he was present when Hudson killed the victim by cutting his throat but a denial that the appellant was responsible for the killing. The judge directed the jury that Ruddock was guilty of murder if he took part in the robbery and knew that there was a possibility that Hudson might intend to kill the victim.

JUDGMENT:- The unanimous conclusion of the court is that Chan Wing-Siu and Powell and English did take a wrong turning and these appeals should therefore be allowed. The correct rule is that foresight is simply evidence, albeit sometimes strong evidence, of intent to assist or encourage, which is the proper mental element for establishing secondary liability.

Authority of Law:-

According to Raz authority means right to tell us what to do or believe. There are two types of authorities, namely, Practical authority which tells us about what to do and Theoretical authority which tells us about what to believe. Authorities mediate between the reasons for action and the subjects of the authority to whom those reasons apply. The directives of the authority have practical importance because they tell the subject how to act so that he does not need directly to consider, at least some of, the reasons that would bear on his acting in the particular circumstance. Arguing against this, Raz says about paradox of authority. This Paradox of authority says that authority is irrational. Everyone should do believe those reasons which make it right thing to do or believe. The Normal Justification thesis says that authority means to act correctly on the balance of reasons, to act on your own assessments on the balance of reasons & not on directions of the authorities.

For example, here, in this case, it is evident that there were two authorities which telling us about what to so & what to believe which are inter-related. The authority says that accessory & principal are both liable for the same charge of offence and accessory's charge will be determined by the charge of principal. This authority has been challenged which we call the paradox of authority. This changed the view of both determining factors of secondary liability in a joint enterprise crime. The UKSC decided that the liability of accessory should not be derived from the liability of its principal. Their intention & knowledge must be same, but in this case accessory wanted to injure or bring harm to Fyfe by smashing the bottle over his head, whereas, the principal stabbed him to death. So, the knowledge & the intention vary here. In this situation, it is immoral to punish accessory for the same charge of his or her principal which deals with the question of practical authority that what to do. Secondly, after getting the judgment of R v Jogee & Ruddock and analytically comparing it with its previous precedents, we can find that the judgment of Jogee & Ruddock changed our views or beliefs on this aspect of secondary liability which deals with the question of theoretical authority.

Exclusionary Reasons:-

Exclusionary reasons are those which authoritative directives that exclude the balance of reasons. Raz believes in Legal Positivism means hard Positivism. Raz considered that hard positivism denies law with morality which is not true at all because positivism develops on natural laws. Natural laws are based on morality. So, positivism cannot separate law from morality. As Raz defined that norms are standard against which human behaviour or other events are assessed. Rules & Orders are norms. Rights of individuals are correlated with duties. Duties are all containing exclusionary reasons. Power is capacity or ability to create, alter and abolish the norm.

For example, here in this case, we can found that UKSC through judicial legislation filled up the gray area left by legislature & earlier precedents and they did it by excluding the balance of reasons that the knowledge & intention of accessory & principal is not in match. So, what punishment is going to be reasonable for the accessory? Is it going to reasonable to punish the accessory simply because he or she was a part of that crime? UKSC used the exclusionary reasons effective which is a part of their duty arising out of their job and used their power to abolish the law created in Powell, English & other previous cases about accessory & principal and create or laid down a new law that if the knowledge & intention is not same, then accessory & principal have to be sued in different charges in accordance with their degree of crime.

Limits of law:-

According to Raz, law has some limitations because of authority. Those limitations are, as follows:

Firstly Limitation:- It must be capable of mediating between the balance of reasons and its subjects. There was a limitation about balance of reason relating to liability of secondary party which UKSC removed by pronouncing the judgment of R v Jogee & Ruddock.

Secondly Limitation:- Mediates to deliberate over the balance of reasons, and then lay down a directive which guides the behaviour of its subjects. R v Jogee & Ruddock has been mediated properly depending upon the balance of reason that degree of crime will determine the liability of accessory.

Third Limitation:- An authoritative directive does not work, if it does tell the subjects what they are to do. In the case the question of directive is not relevant because the error was in the precedent & gray area was left by the legislature while enacting statutes.

Fourth Limitation:- If a directive requires the subject to determine for themselves what 'the law' requires, then the law is not being authoritative, and such a directive would not count as law. In the case the question of directive is not relevant because the error was in the precedent & gray area was left by the legislature while enacting statutes.

Fifth Limitation:- The law may require its subjects to act 'fairly and reasonably' in certain circumstances. In the case of Powell, the law was very unfair because one who is bringing the charge against someone, must prove his or her case. Otherwise, accusing other will be a rule and that cannot bring peace in any society. In Powell, prosecution failed to prove the case, but the offender got punished which is neither fair nor reasonable. Secondly, in Powell's case, the intention & knowledge of party has not been judged clearly like the case of Jogee. In Jogee, we know that the principal & the accessory had same intention to bring harm or injury to Fyfe, but there was a difference opinion between them about with what instrument they are going to bring harm or injury to Fyfe. This clarifies the degree of liability of crime and fairness & reasonableness. This scenario is absent from Powell's case, but this limitation has been corrected by R v Jogee & Ruddock.

Sixth Limitation:- An authority cannot direct behaviour if the behaviour it wants to direct cannot be specified, thus the problem is the general one of the law's making reference in its authoritative directives to issues or matters which can only be dealt with by further deliberation. For example, in the case of Powell, what gang member behave in what way was not proved by the prosecution. So, the authority must not direct anything in this situation. This limitation has been also cured by the judgment of R v Jogee & Ruddock.

Seventh Limitation:- Such directives necessarily fail to allow the subject to proceed to the executive phase of practical reason, in which case, they are not truly authoritative directives. Indeed, the authority we had before R v Jogee & Ruddock's case was not truly authority because if punishment required for reformation from criminality & to bring back to normal societal life which need to be decided on intention. If the intention has not been proved like Powell's case, then there is no true authority.

Eighth Limitation:- The most such directives can do in a system of regulation such as the law is to empower judges to make actual orders in cases or, if they are entitled to make law, lay down actual, workable, directives within the constraints of the power. For example, the judicial legislation made in the case of R v Jogee & Ruddock which corrected the limitation of earlier precedents of liability of secondary party in any joint enterprise crime.

Separation Theory:-

The Theory of separation says that there must be an adequate test for the existence and content of law must be based only on social facts, and not moral arguments. Law and morality are conceptually distinct. It is true that some social rulings had not develop on morality, but those authorities can be tested before court of law. As Dworkin said that pre-interpretative, some authorities have no value attached to the morality. At interpretative stage, this can be challenged and at post-interpretative stage a new authority born depending upon morality which changes the pre-interpretative stage. Also the paradox of authority theory provided Raz speaks against this view that authorities has to be tested through reasons and reasons are always based on morality.

I cannot agree much with the view of this separation theory of Raz because law & morals are not much different & both are interrelated. For example, in the case of Jogee, we have enough social faces that the accessory & the principal got drunk & went to Fyfe's home to bring harm or injury to other. So, what next we need to do when these social facts are lies at our hands? We need to apply our reasonable thinking and decide were they right and are those actions going to bring peace in our society or not. This is known as moral thinking. So, social facts throw us to think morally and this is the one of the reason for which separation theory cannot be supported.

Exclusive Legal Positivism:-

Three features characterize courts of law:

- Firstly, they deal with disputes with the aim of resolving them.

- Secondly, they issue authoritative rulings which decide these disputes.
- Thirdly, in their activities they are bound to be guided, at least partly, by positivist authoritative considerations.

The first point does not imply that courts of law do not engage in other activities than settling disputes. This true absolutely because court has to resolve disputes depending on relevancy of facts & question of laws and if other activities are relevant, then court of law considers that. The second limb of the above definition of a court of law like it issues authoritative rulings and these rulings can be tested by appellate forums of court which has no end. The concept of lager bench ensures that unless a dispute being resolved and no-one is challenging that issue further, larger bench can be constituted to test those principles.

For example, in the case of R v Jogee & Ruddock, firstly, UKSC were involved to resolve the dispute about the liability of accessory & principal in a crime of joint enterprise. Secondly, the judgment of R v Jogee & Ruddock is authoritative in the field of secondary liability in complicity now which will govern the minimum standard of punishment relating to this crime, until & unless it goes obsolete or overruled. Finally, even though the judgments of Powell & English were wrong in deciding the principles of liability of secondary party, but it was the guiding factor until Jogee & Ruddock decided.

Negligence from Raz:-

Critics says that the theory of Raz neglects those social problems that Social problems that law deals with that cannot or should not be solved by authority.

- Firstly, this statement is not true at all because there is no problem which cannot be solved by authority. If authorities are wrong or immoral, then that can be challenged, but there cannot be any problem without solution.
- Secondly, if we follow the restricted way of interpretation of hard positivism, then it is true that authorities cannot solve social problems. From this perspective, Raz is correct. On the contrary, we can say that law is a scheme of justice which flows like river with the development through

time. Hard positivism cannot change with the flow of development through time, but soft positivism can always change. It is evident that Raz, speaks about authority of hard positivism and the rigidity of which indeed cannot solve some social problem by authority. It is true that the theory of Raz neglected the balanced view of authority.

For example, in the case of Powell & English, we can find that social problems were neglected because prosecution failed to prove the charges against accessory & principal separately and House of Lords held guilty all accessories & principal, depending upon that, but this is not the circumstances of every case. In the case of Jogee & Ruddock, we can find that UKSC devoted a lot time decide the principle. It is not true that Raz's theory deals only with those problems which cannot be dealt with or solved by authority. His theory is concerned about authority in general & its impact upon law and morality.

Dworkin's theory of Morality:-

Dworkin's interpretative theory provide two types of interpretation to us, firstly, hard positivism where he says that judges must not derive from the letters of the law and secondly, soft positivism which says that if the case is hard case and there is a gray area, then judges can decide that case going beyond the letters of law. This idea speaks that every authority can be challenged and tested in court. Dworkin and Raz differed on another view that Raz said that rule and principle and policies are not categorically different. According to Dworkin, rules and principles are not categorically different because both of them are our rights, but policies are community goals which are different from principles. Here, Raz cannot be supported because both, policies and principles can be challenged before court of laws and those can be set aside if that is not made for the welfare of the society.

For example, if Jogee's case has not challenged or decided by UKSC, then English courts had to follow the rulings of statues which was unclear about liability of secondary crime and lead to vary from case to case that cannot bring coherence or consistency or on the other hand have to follow the precedent of Powell, English or other previous precedents which took wrong turning on this aspect. This can lead to frustration to increase in crime, civil war and finally, no peaceful society, but challenging this doctrine of liability of secondary party through the case of Jogee & Ruddock, was extremely helpful to correct the decision. here, Dworkin is right about his criticism relating to Raz's authority of law.

Conclusion:-

We can conclude by saying that Raz, being strictly sticking to his theory of hard positivism, neglected the balanced view of authority.

References:-

- https://treasuryofenglishlaws.wordpress.com/2019/04/10/razs-authority-of-law/

<u>Anything to note?</u>

Grundnorm by Kelsen

Issue:-

Kelsen's theory of Grundnorm or Pure theory of law is not a balanced view of law because it only focused on the coerciveness of legal norm. Hart's theory is more convincing than him because Hart focuses on both soft & hard positivism. Raz's criticism of Kelsen is very meaningful because he pointed out that which Kelsen lacks about the authority that denotes the concept oughtness.

Case Study: R v Jogee & R v Ruddock:-

ISSUE:- The question of law was whether the common law took a wrong turning in two cases, Chan Wing-Siu v The Queen and Regina v Powell and English.

FACTS:- The appellant Jogee was convicted at Nottingham Crown Court of the murder of Paul Fyfe. Mr Fyfe was the boyfriend of Naomi Reid and he was stabbed to death in the hallway of her home in the early hours of 10 June 2011 by the appellant's co-defendant, Mohammed Hirsi. Hirsi was convicted of murder. The appellant and Hirsi spent the previous evening at various places, taking drink and drugs. They became increasingly intoxicated and increasingly aggressive. Shortly before midnight they arrived at Ms Reid's house. She told them to leave and They left but Hirsi returned and was there when Mr Fyfe arrived. Hirsi entered the house and there was an angry confrontation between him and Mr Fyfe. The appellant was outside with a bottle and shouting to Hirsi to do something to Mr Fyfe and at one stage the appellant came to the door and threatened to smash the bottle over Mr Fyfe's head. The fatal stabbing was done by Hirsi with a knife which he took from the kitchen. The judge directed the jury that the appellant was guilty of murder if he took part in the attack on Mr Fyfe and realised that it was possible that Hirsi might use the knife with intent to cause serious harm. The appellant Ruddock was convicted in the Circuit Court at

Montego Bay, Jamaica, of the murder of Peter Robinson. The appellant's co-defendant, Hudson, pleaded guilty to the murder. Mr Robinson was a taxi driver and the prosecution's case was that the murder was committed in the course of robbing him of his station wagon. The police evidence was that the appellant made a statement under caution which amounted to an admission that he was involved in committing the robbery and that he was present when Hudson killed the victim by cutting his throat but a denial that the appellant was responsible for the killing. The judge directed the jury that Ruddock was guilty of murder if he took part in the robbery and knew that there was a possibility that Hudson might intend to kill the victim.

JUDGMENT:- The unanimous conclusion of the court is that Chan Wing-Siu and Powell and English did take a wrong turning and these appeals should therefore be allowed. The correct rule is that foresight is simply evidence, albeit sometimes strong evidence, of intent to assist or encourage, which is the proper mental element for establishing secondary liability.

Pure Theory of Law:-

Grundnorm is a German work which basically means foundation of norm or basic norm. This denotes as the ultimate norm that confer validity upon norms which is speaking about the constitution. Pure Theory means that description of law is different from what the law to be, even though it has an ought proposition with it. The pure theory recommends that all positive law should be viewed as a system of norms stipulating that, under certain conditions. Norms are generally action-directing means duty imposing by power or permission. This is different than moral norms which are the subjective preferences for behaviour. This theory has a limited effect in United Kingdom because we do not have any codified constitution.

Here, in this case, we can found that violating criminal's right for charging him or her for higher offeces are violation of human rights which has its foundation since

1215 through the great charter of Magna Carta. Adversarial litigation system were developed on 18th century by William Garrow. Historically, there was a death trap at Old Bailey at 18th century where generally cases took no longer than 15 minutes to be decided. It was a convention at that period that innocent should be able to argue their own cases. The Bloody Code interpreted that you must not be punished for stealing houses, but the horses must not be stolen and for this reason the law must punish the offender. Pious perjury had a great role to play then when juries were enshrined to go against with their oath to bring true verdict by either to find people not guilty & more often reduced the amount of property stolen, so property crime will be no longer a capital offence. Until this period, barrister's roles were restricted to civil laws, but by 18th century barristers started to prosecute criminal cases on behalf of the crown. William Garrow gave birth to this system of adversarial litigation system and this shifted the principle of presentation of the case made by the prosecution than traditionally which was focused on charges against the accused. This principle of adversarial litigation system can be found in Jogee & Ruddock's case that their intention & knowledge must be presented to court properly by their barristers which will decide their charge of committed offence. Trial was no longer a test against defendants from 18th century like Anglo-Saxon or Norman period, but a test of evidence which need to be prove beyond every doubt. It is the presumption of innocence until proven guilty which in the case of Powell, English & earlier cases failed to recognise the liability of secondary party separately from its principal offender in any joint enterprise crime.

Sanctions by Officials:-

Kelsen said that there were two things universally true of law:

- Firstly, that it was coercive, and
- Secondly, that it was a system of norms.

For a legal norm to be described as 'valid' it must be a member of a system. According to Kelsen, moral judgments are irrational. He also says that Fact cannot gather norm. Legal norms are coercion by systematic use of sanctions, applied by agents or officials. Unique about law is coercion & offialdom. Kelsen introduced another German idea that is Delicto which means in the act of committing an offence, officials can impose sanction which is not immoral. According to Kelsen, secondary norms are as genuine as primary norm, for example, sanctions by officials.

To contradict & prove Kelsen wrong, I want to discuss the case of Jogee & Ruddock here. Kelsen said fact cannot gather norm, moral judgments are irrational. In the case of Powell when prosecution failed to prove the case, then holding accessory liable for the same charge as his or her principal done is wrong, but when we have facts in our hand that Powell with his gang murdered a drug dealer or Jogee & hirshi went to the house of Fyfe with prior planning to bring harm or injury to him, then we think that those actions were right or wrong which forms norm. If we do not have those facts in our hand, then we do not think what is right or what is wrong. So, Kelsen is wrong that fact cannot gather norms. Fact is the basis of formation of norms. Secondly, moral judgments cannot be irrational because human being is rational being. Their cognitive thinking made them rational being and the basis of this cognitive thinking is morality or formation of guilty mind. This guilty mind tells us that what is ought to be right or what is ought to be as wrong. Sometimes, people made error in interpreting them. For example, in the case of Powell there was an error that prosecution fails to prove the case, then instead giving an acquittal, House of Lords decided that accessories are liable for the same amount of crime as his or her principal does, but this does means that moral judgments are irrational because in the case of R v Jogee & Ruddock, UKSC pronounced its judgment, depending upon morality. So, morality or guilty mind or cognition which made us rational being, that can never be irrational, if rational thinking have interpreted in properly and without having any error in it.

The mythology & Obscurity in Kelsen:-

It says that the Transcendental-Logical condition of this normative interpretation, does not perform an ethical-political but it do perform an epistemological function. According to Kelsen, Transcendental means outside and independent from experience of facts with which we cannot agree because if any law is outside than facts, then that would be unrealistic. He describes Normativity as a matter of rules. Performing an ethical-political function means for Kelsen that it is making an evaluative statement of morality or politics. So, the Epistemological means making clear how we can know something.

For example, in the case of Powell, we can find that law is going outside of facts because prosecution did not proved who murdered the drug dealer and how other member of that gang interacted with them, but in the later case of R v Jogee & Ruddock, it was decided that Powell, English & other previous cases took a wrong turning. Accessory must know in what way principal is going to commit the crime and that must be supported with proper intention which can hold the accessory liable same as the principal. This case of Jogee & Ruddock proved that if law goes outside facts, then that is bad and liable to be set-aside or overruled by subsequent cases.

Neo-Kantian Basic Norm:-

Paulson and Harris described Grundnorm as transcendental presupposition which has three ingredients, are as follows:
- Firstly, we form knowledge of valid legal norms which has objective normative force. Objective normative force means laws deriving from oughtness.

- Secondly, for this to be possible, we must presuppose the category of the basic norm.
- Thirdly, because we must presuppose it, then the basic norm is true.

For example, here in case, we can find that we form our knowledge of liability of secondary party in a joint enterprise crime from the case or the law or precedent or norm decided at R v Jogee & Ruddock. The oughtness decided in the case about the liability of accessory has the objective normative force. This objective normative force must be presupposed as the category of basic norm means the constitution. United Kingdom has no one codified constitution, but it has several written constitutional documents. Violating accessory's right by punishing him or her for higher offence means violating the human rights of accessory and human right is our constitutional document. So, the judgment of Jogee & Ruddock can be presupposed as the category of basic norm because it proved the constructional norms have true existence in our society.

Criticism of Kelsen:-

The unity of Kelsen's theory says that Kelsen was wrong that all laws are directed to officials, who are required to apply sanctions. For example, international laws are normative in nature. International laws are like contractual laws. It's terms & conditions are binding and the parties are binding themselves. So, it is not always true that we need officials who can apply sanctions which can make laws as law. The most possible redundancy of the Grundnorm is as Austin's theory says that it wrongly derived that oughts of law from the fact of habitual obedience to a sovereign. The oughtness or normativity of law is bound up in the idea of the basic norm.

This has no applicability in the case of R V Jogee & Ruddock because institutions of United Kingdom are applying the sanction against a crime done by Jogee & Hisrhi. The degree of liability is question which is not coming under the purview of this criticism.

Hart Convincing than Kelsen:-

Hart's theory is more convincing than Kelsen because Kelsen only focused on laws which are sanctioned by officials. According to Hart, the social practice or the rule of recognition is the normative order which is independent from morality & fact. Kelsen's basic norm is not identified as a matter of fact but is, rather, a presupposition that certain rules are valid, presupposes laws to be valid. Kelsen ignored the rule of recognition's factual existence as a test of validity. There are two general principles required to be understand to know Kelsen:

- Firstly, the basic norm is that coercive acts ought to be done by officials, in accordance with the constitution which considered as first historically. It is not the fact of the first constitution, the constitution itself is the basic norm, because the constitution is a fact, not a norm. Rather, the basic norm is: acts ought to be done in accordance with the constitution. Kelsen said that constitution is a fact & not a norm. If constitution is a fact & not a norm, then it cannot bind every laws of any country. Facts are not binding. Facts give raise the question of morality and that give raise to natural and ultimately positive law. Constitution upholds the rights of people or citizens of any country. It is a positive law itself derived from natural laws which depend solely on oughtness or morality. Kelsen's view cannot be supported here because neither constitution is a fact nor laws are coercive in nature. For example, distributive justice, family laws, contract laws. In all these branch of laws we cannot show the coercive nature of law as Kelsen described it.
- Secondly, Effectiveness is not a sufficient condition for the validity of a legal order, but it is a necessary condition. Indeed, effectiveness is a necessary condition and also it is not sufficient. Here, we cannot disagree with Kelsen at all.

For example, is our constitutional sources are considered as mere facts & norms, then there will be no violation of human rights for accessories like Jogee, if they hold guilty for higher offences. Historically, defendant has rights of defence and this culture of rights invented by Thomas Erskine in England on 18th century. Rights of defence include right to defend to be charged for proper offences which can give protection to be punished for higher charge of offence. If constitution is face & not a norm and accessory like Jogee has no human rights, then it is evident that right of defence does not exist there. This is contrary to the principles of adversarial litigation system as well as British constitution. On this point Kelsen can never be supported because if other laws are have to be governed in accordance with constitution, then constitution must have the force to compel them when they are at disobedience. This character of constitution makes it the basic norm & not leaving it as only a fact.

Criticism by Raz:-

Raz also believed in authority, but his view is more preferable than Kelsen. According to Raz norms are a fixed standard against which human behaviour or other events are assessed. Raz's famous normal justification thesis says that an authority is legitimate means the subjects of the authority are justified in its guidance, and an authority is justified in issuing directives to guide the behaviour of those subject to it, when those subjects are more likely to comply with the reasons that ought to govern their behaviour if they follow the directives of the authority than if they were to try themselves to follow those reasons directly. Law can be coercive with reason and reason is morality. Furthermore, Raz states that Parochial concepts are concepts which cannot be mastered by all, not even by everyone capable of knowledge. 'Non-parochial' concepts can be mastered by anyone capable of knowing anything at all. The acquisition of certain parochial concepts will depend upon having certain perceptual capabilities, but our chief concern here are parochial evaluative concepts, and the way in which access to certain evaluative concepts may depend upon one's living in cultural circumstances which create, sustain, or provide access to certain values. To the extent that one's exposure to these values is contingent in the sense that they depend upon one's being in or sufficiently related to a particular culture, the concepts of those values are parochial. Kelsen speaks about Grundnorm which is not universal, but true for his community.

For example, Accessories & Abettor's Act 1861 is a fixed standard of norm. We have to decided the liability of secondary party in light of this statute, but if any gray found in it, then precedents like Powell, English & other cases are becoming the guiding factor as fixed norms, but when it was pointed that those guiding factors also contain gray area, then R v Jogee & Ruddock's case UKSC became desperate settle this disputed issue in question of liability of accessory. Norms are always there which determines the standard of behaviour. When these norms are tested through judicial decision, then those are called rule of law. Secondly, Kelsen is contradicting with himself because he said that constitution is fact and fact cannot gather norms, if fact cannot gather norms then it is contradicting that how other norms can be decided in accordance with constitutional principle. Raz's theory has some meaningful foundation, but rigid in nature, whereas, Kelsen's theory cannot be supported at least at English legal System at all.

Conclusion:-

We can conclude that Kelsen's pure theory of law is not a balanced view of what law is or what it ought to be because it speaks about some wings of law which are coercive in nature, but those laws can never treated as laws if they lack morality or reason in it.

References:-

- https://treasuryofenglishlaws.wordpress.com/2019/04/11/grundnorm-of-kelsen/

<u>*Anything to note?*</u>

Derive is from Ought

Issue:-

The issue that "No Is can be derived from any Ought" is merely an anti-positivism statement and baseless or not. Anti-Positivist says that law or courts should not derive is from ought which overtime, became obsolete. Currently, law reform committee's are acting to find out what law ought to be and legislation enact laws depending upon morality and finally, courts are deciding what the law is or should be deriving from what ought to be where the law is left uncertain by the legislature. In this case of R v jogee & Ruddock, the UKSC decided the "IS" deriving from the "OUGHT".

Case Study: R v Jogee & R v Ruddock:-

ISSUE:- The question of law was whether the common law took a wrong turning in two cases, Chan Wing-Siu v The Queen and Regina v Powell and English.

FACTS:- The appellant Jogee was convicted at Nottingham Crown Court of the murder of Paul Fyfe. Mr Fyfe was the boyfriend of Naomi Reid and he was stabbed to death in the hallway of her home in the early hours of 10 June 2011 by the appellant's co-defendant, Mohammed Hirsi. Hirsi was convicted of murder. The appellant and Hirsi spent the previous evening at various places, taking drink and drugs. They became increasingly intoxicated and increasingly aggressive. Shortly before midnight they arrived at Ms Reid's house. She told them to leave and They left but Hirsi returned and was there when Mr Fyfe arrived. Hirsi entered the house and there was an angry confrontation between him and Mr Fyfe. The appellant was outside with a bottle and shouting to Hirsi to do something to Mr Fyfe and at one stage the appellant came to the door and threatened to smash the bottle over Mr Fyfe's head. The fatal stabbing was done by Hirsi with a knife which he took from the kitchen. The judge directed the jury that the appellant was guilty of murder if he took part in the attack on Mr Fyfe and realised that it was possible that Hirsi might use the knife with intent to cause serious harm. The appellant Ruddock was convicted in the Circuit Court at

Montego Bay, Jamaica, of the murder of Peter Robinson. The appellant's co-defendant, Hudson, pleaded guilty to the murder. Mr Robinson was a taxi driver and the prosecution's case was that the murder was committed in the course of robbing him of his station wagon. The police evidence was that the appellant made a statement under caution which amounted to an admission that he was involved in committing the robbery and that he was present when Hudson killed the victim by cutting his throat but a denial that the appellant was responsible for the killing. The judge directed the jury that Ruddock was guilty of murder if he took part in the robbery and knew that there was a possibility that Hudson might intend to kill the victim.

JUDGMENT:- The unanimous conclusion of the court is that Chan Wing-Siu and Powell and English did take a wrong turning and these appeals should therefore be allowed. The correct rule is that foresight is simply evidence, albeit sometimes strong evidence, of intent to assist or encourage, which is the proper mental element for establishing secondary liability.

What is Ought:-

Ought is not only always morality, but also is the reason and justification that lies behind evolution. Positivism doesn't include morality in law. They think that Law can be morally problematic. Law means what the law is than it is ought to be. Legal Positivism theory denotes that the 'is' and the moral 'ought' of law are separate from each other. Positivism stood for the doctrine that it does not follow that if something is law, it is, therefore, morally right. Coercive acts ought to be performed under the conditions and in the manner which the historically the constitution, and the norms created according to it, prescribe. Professor Simmonds says that Law claims to guide and to justify our conduct: it purports to impose obligations upon us, and to tell us what we "ought" to do. Judges invoke legal rules as a justification for their decisions or decisions that may order the use of coercive measures such as punishment.

For example, here in the case of R v Jogee & Ruddock, the UKSC decided that what ought to be the liability of secondary party while committing any crime. The standard of liability that accessory must not be punished for the same offence as the principal, if knowledge & intention differs, as it happen in this case, is based on OUGHT. If Is cannot be derived from Ought, then UKSC had to follow what decided already in Powell, English & all other previous cases.

Positivist Jurists:-

Historically, legal theory started to begin with Plato, Aristotle, Scotics or how ought a man to live. Legal theory was described as that law is practical application of morality. Bentham's critique of natural law is based on the modern jurisprudence debate including:

- Firstly, the question of separation of law and as it ought to be, the concept of law for positivists is a concept with no intrinsic moral connotations and secondly is the question of how we are to conceive of the nature of legal standards. H.L.A. Hart's Linguistic Method or Linguistic Philosophy says that primary rules are concerned with being obliged or forced or duty imposing by the sovereign. Whereas the secondary rules are concern with being under an obligation or ought to be obliged under the Idea of Obligation. Social practice or Rule of recognition or Normative order is independent from morality & fact. Furthermore, Hart says that where an accepted rules exist, the regular pattern of conforming behaviour or the external aspect is accompanied by an internal aspect; Internal point of view as a reason for action. Ought to be done or treated as imposing obligation or as conferring rights. For example, here in this case, there gray area in primary legislation. Powell, English & previous cases requires force of sovereignty to have habitual obedience because those cases lacks proper reasoning. In deciding the case of Jogee, the UKSC followed the Ought reasoning or the internal point of view of professor Hart which viewed as reason for action. This judgment of R v Jogee & Ruddock imposes an obligation that in degree of knowledge and intention varies, then accessory will not go unpunished and wrongful acts will still be wrongful, but he has to be tried for proper charge of offence. This principle also it contain right in it that whether Jogee wanted to murder Fyfe or not is unclear, but he wanted to bring harm to him which is a wrongful act. So, accessory must be punished, but he has a right to defend himself, if the prosecution is going to bring higher charges against him at trial.

- Secondly, Raz argued that when those subjects are more likely to comply with the reasons that ought to govern their behaviour which they follow the directives of the authority, than if they were to try themselves to follow those reasons directly. For example, it is known to everyone in England & Wales that bringing harm & injury to other is an offence, but it is difficult to understand what is wrongful, if there is no authority. In the case of R v Jogee & Ruddock, UKSC set the standard of liability of secondary party, depending upon reasons. A reasonable man can be expected to understand the reasons which will bring automatic changes to his beviour as Raz identified.

- Finally, Liberal feminism argues that the basic beliefs of political liberalism that human beings are rational and autonomous and ought to be treated equally to apply to women as well as to men. Julie Dickson said that The first 'stage' of our inquiries into the character of law ought not to be morally evaluative, and certainly ought not to be morally commendatory or justificatory in its approach and Instead, this 'first stage' of legal philosophical inquiry involves identifying, selecting and explaining law's important and significant features. Even though this case of Jogee & Ruddock is not relevant as an example of feminism, I want to bring one different thought of mine here that Fyfe's girlfriend is a woman. Losing of loved one by Jogee & Hirshi, cannot be compensated neither by way of fine nor imprisonment, but everyone must be treated equally. She has a right that she has been injured emotionally because of losing Fyfe. Punishing offenders can bring a little relief, but if accessory has been punished for higher offence, then that will another scare in her mind that when he will be out from imprisonment, he will became more aggressive for that higher punishment and will try to bring harm or injury to her or other in out peaceful society again.

Higher punishment is the other form of injustice which can never bring peace to any society or bring justice to either party of any crime.

Anti-Positivist jurists:-

Hume found that there seems to be a significant difference between positive statements means about what is and prescriptive or normative statements means about what ought to be, and that it is not obvious how one can coherently move from descriptive statements to prescriptive ones. Natural Fallacy of Finnis says that Natural rights are what ought to be and that *"no is can be derived from an Ought"*. Kelsen's Pure Theory says that description of law is different from what the law to be, even though it has ought proposition. Austin's theory wrongly derived 'oughts' of law from the 'is's' of the fact of habitual obedience to a sovereign. 'Oughtness' or normativity of law is bound up in the idea of the basic norm. The basic norm is that coercive acts ought to be done by officials, in accordance with the historically first constitution; it is not the fact of the first constitution, the constitution itself is the basic norm, because the constitution is a fact, not a norm. Rather, the basic norm is: acts ought to be done in accordance with the constitution.

Here, I am absolutely disagreeing with David Hume and to prove that one can move from descriptive statements to prescriptive ones, I want to discuss about why people so or involve in crime in light of the brain structure of human being here which is the best evolution in the universe, known to us.

Crime & Brain:-

The best answer of why people involve in crime has three issues:

- **_Codification Problem:-_** We forget what is right & what is wrongful because human brain may absent when encoding that information. No necessary that everyone has to be a student of law to understand what is treated as crime & what is not. Anything can give us this information that what is right & is wrong. Encoding that information properly is the first problem. Then retaining that information and decoding at proper moment are not an easy think thing to do, but reasonable people who have a kind heart can easily use reasoning and become successful in many occasions.
- **_Emotions:-_** This is the main cause of crime. We feel for something which leads us to seeking that in our lives as our choice of entertainment. When we cannot get that we became aggressive. Controlling emotion can reduce the rate of crime extensively and this can be done best through CBT means Cognitive Behavioral therapy treatment.

- ***Sleep:-*** Deprivation of sleep causes mental disorder. Micro-Sleep or Sleep-Deprivation can cause everything from sleep walking, sleep-talking, Insomnia which is dangerous for driving, Obesity, Anxiety disorder, whereas, Long-Sleep is associated with inflammation which is an immune response linked from depression to heart disease. Some of these are used as defence under criminal law which includes:
  - ***Brain Damage:-*** Either for psychological or physical damage of the brain people forget what is a prohibited act out of aggressiveness. For example, automatism. These defences can save to be punished because this damage in brain can paralysis our reasonable thinking for a particular specific time or for long time.
  - ***Compel to do crime:-*** Sometimes people are compel to crime. For Example, self-defence.

For example, here in this case, we can find that Jogee & Hirshi are both, reasonable people. So, here codification problem is fitting best that Jogee & Hirshi were drunk because they give themselves the dutch courage throughout the evening to do the crime which is no defence. Secondly, in that drunkenness they could not recall or decode that bringing harm or injury to others are prohibited in law, but Jogee still had no intention to murder Fyfe. He just encouraged to smash the bottle over Fyfe's head. In this situation if UKSC punish Jogee for murder which he did not commit, then that would be an injustice done to him which can cause frustration to his mind. This frustration can cause pain in his brain which pain can bring chemical changes first to his brain and spread throughout the whole body. Finally, this chemical change can do two types of harm, one is either to himself or the other is against his society. So, if Is cannot be derived from Ought or one cannot move from descriptive statements to prescriptive ones, then that will increase crime out of frustration.

Where Anti-Positivist Jurists Fails:-

If we consider the Rome & Greek rulings, then we can find one ruler is ruling a huge population in accordance with his desire and not depending upon morality. When that goes extreme, an outburst leads to the end of that dynasty which we call civil war or revolution. At that period, indeed, law did not contain any morality in law, but from 13th century onwards when law profession started to develop in England, then it started to develop, depending upon morality. From 16th century with the development of separation of power, put the final pin to the concept of law with morality. Parliament is sovereign and elected because its prime purpose is to defend the rights of citizens and when they fails or executive fails to uphold the right of citizens or its people, then judiciary as an expert body decide what is the fault in the law and how that ought to be removed. This brings morality into positivism which anti-positivist jurists are unable to consider.

For example, here in this case, we can find that UKSC said that Powell, English & other previous cases took a wrong turning in deciding the amount of liability of secondary party. This checks-n-balance was available before 13th century. At that period we can say that is cannot be derived from ought or no-one should go from descriptive statements to prescriptive ones, but at this 21st century this thinking has become obsolete purely.

Prescriptive Theory:-

Prescriptive Thesis deals with what court ought to do. If we consider the Article 9 of ECHR because European Union is an international origination and international law is based on normative law which speaks about "what ought to be". International law is agreed behaviour about how countries ought to behave because from ancient period to WW-II, it is evident that many countries are encroaching upon the rights of other country. When conflict of laws develops, then problems became more complicated.

Here, in the case of R v Jogee & Ruddock, the UKSC uphold the human rights of accessory properly and in accordance with Oughtness. If UKSC fails to do so & Jogee moved his case before ECtHR, then ECtHR can hold that our domestic laws are in contradiction with the basis of international law & English laws are failing to comply with international obligation by not upholding the right of the defendant properly, but by deciding through morality and deriving is from ought UKSC changed the view of English laws worldwide.

Descriptive theory:-

Descriptive Thesis deals with what courts actually do. Court decide the aspect of what law is based on ought, but critics says that what courts actually do is different than what ought to be done.

For example, if we consider Powell's case, then it is true that what courts actually do is different than what ought to be done because prosecution fails to prove that who committed the crime, then it is not proper to hold that the accessory must liable for same amount of crime as the principal. On the contrary, if we consider the later case of R v Jogee or Ruddock, then we can find that court decided the liability of secondary party depending purely upon ought principle. So, It is evident that courts are not deciding cases differently from morality where there is any uncertainty lies in the law. Sometimes, failure of interpretation of fact or situation of crime and analysing that fact in light of law can lead to absurdity, but that does not mean the crisis is sacrosanct.

Is-Ought Solution:-

According to professor Hart internal aspect is ought to be complied with. Internal aspect of this case was that Jogee did not have intention to stab Fyfe with knife or he did not know that Hirshi is going to stab Fyfe immediately. So, applying the internal aspect or the moral reason here, the UKSC decided properly that "IT IS MORAL TO PUNISH THE ACCESSORY FOR THE OFFENCE AGAINST WHICH OUGHT TO BE PUNISHED IN ACCORDANCE WITH LAW".

Conclusion:-

We can conclude by saying that it is not true that "no is can be derived from an ought" and proudly move from descriptive statements to prescriptive ones.

References:-

- How Your Brain Works by New Scientist Instant Expert;
- https://treasuryofenglishlaws.wordpress.com/2019/04/26/derive-is-from-ought/

<u>*Anything to note?*</u>

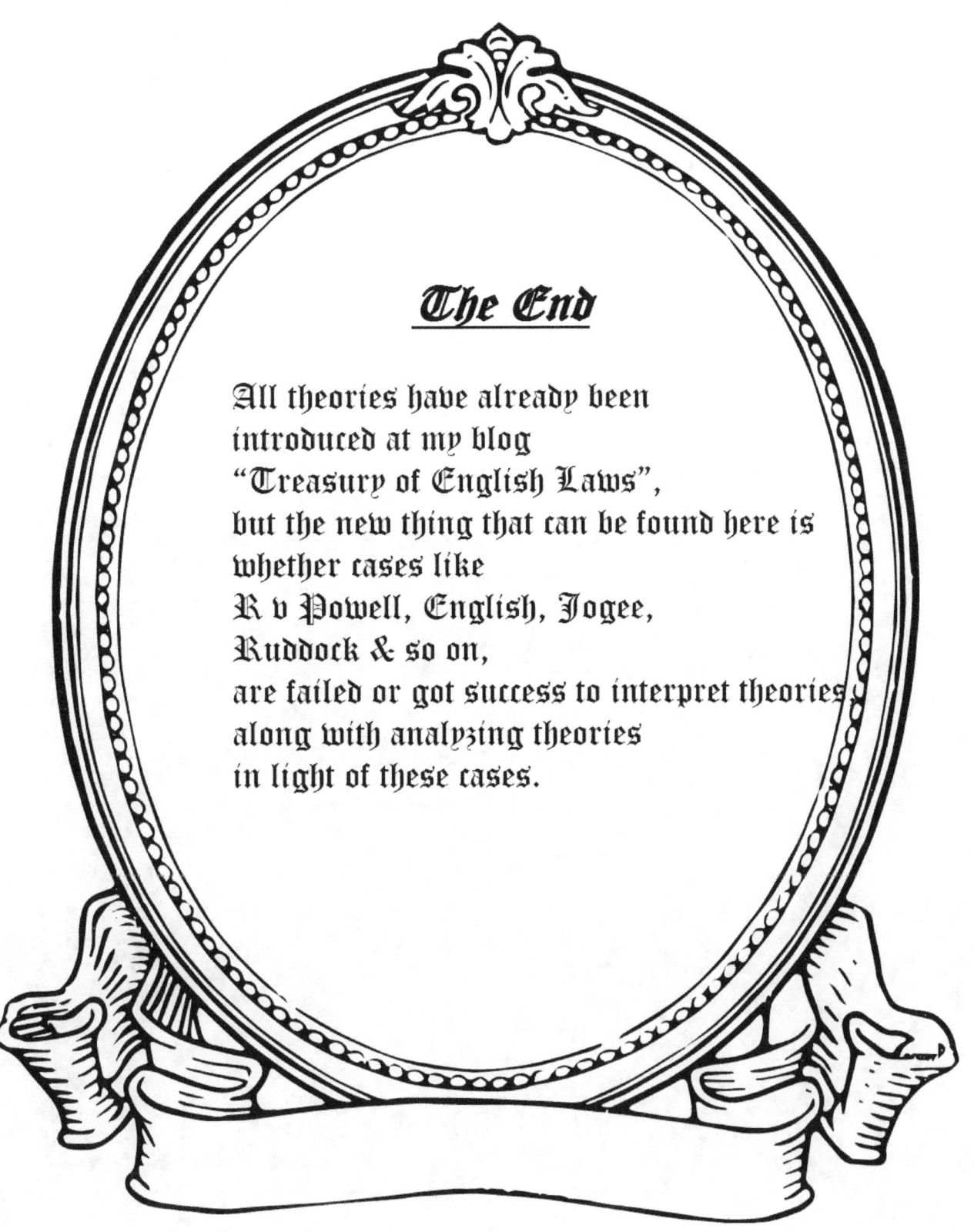

The End

All theories have already been
introduced at my blog
"Treasury of English Laws",
but the new thing that can be found here is
whether cases like
R v Powell, English, Jogee,
Ruddock & so on,
are failed or got success to interpret theories
along with analyzing theories
in light of these cases.

www.ingramcontent.com/pod-product-compliance
Lightning Source LLC
Chambersburg PA
CBHW081006170526
45158CB00010B/2928